The Good News Is Love

The Good News Is Love

by
Mary Marrocco

Saint Mary's Press
Christian Brothers Publications
Winona, Minnesota

To Dad and Mother,
because of whom
I need never wonder
whether love is true

Genuine recycled paper with 10% post-consumer waste.
Printed with soy-based ink.

The publishing team included Carl Koch, development editor; Laurie A. Berg, copy editor; Barbara Bartelson, production editor and typesetter; Maurine R. Twait, art director and cover designer; cover photo, © PhotoDisc Inc.; pre-press, printing, and binding by the graphics division of Saint Mary's Press.

Printed in the United States of America

Printing: 9 8 7 6 5 4 3 2 1

Year: 2006 05 04 03 02 01 00 99 98

ISBN 0-88489-503-3

Contents

Introduction *7*

Matthew 11:28–30
Easy? You Call Love Easy? *12*

Mark 2:1–12
Faith Makes an Opening *17*

Luke 9:43–51
Let This Sink In *21*

John 1:35–51
Come and Get It *26*

Acts of the Apostles 5:40–42
Cause for Rejoicing *30*

Acts of the Apostles 9:1–19
Breathing Fire *35*

Acts of the Apostles 23:1–11
Courage *40*

2 Corinthians 4:1–12
Brighter and Brighter *45*

2 Corinthians 12:1–10
Perfect in Weakness *50*

Ephesians 5:8–20
The Light of Love *54*

Philippians 3:7–14
Wanting *58*

Colossians 3:1–4
Back to Life *64*

1 Thessalonians 4:13–18
To Dream a Little *70*

1 Peter 5:6–11
Cast Your Cares *75*

2 Peter 1:16–21
The Morning Star Rises *80*

Introduction

The Good News. The Scriptures. The Holy Bible. The word of God. This book is written to help you come closer to that great book, and so to the God whose gift it is.

The central message of the Scriptures is love. The word of God became flesh in the humanity of Jesus to show God's infinitely patient, always faithful, powerfully tender love for us. Jesus healed, preached, forgave, and loved us to his death on the cross. Of course Jesus' love story did not end there. Christ rose from the tomb, conquering death and promising resurrection. In love the Holy Spirit abides with us now, drawing us to truth, inviting us to hope, and gracing us to love. The good news is love.

Whether you have hardly ever read the Bible or you have a profound appreciation for it, this book offers one way of hearing the good news that is love. It is designed to help you enter into the conversation between the loving God and us. That conversation is spoken in Christ, who is the Word of God. To come closer to the Bible is to come closer to Christ and to the people whom Christ has gathered. The spirit of God never leaves us orphans, but draws us through encounters with the word to communion with the whole Body of Christ.

Every word in the Bible is a word of love and a meeting place between God and God's beloved. Each Scripture passage included in this book is a private place where you and the One who loves you can meet together in honesty and intimacy, a secret garden filled with unknown flowers. The passages have been chosen from various books of the Christian Testament, rather as one might pick different types of flowers from the garden so as to sample the variety of scents and colors. The aim is to invite you further into each Christian Testament book represented here and to help you walk into that garden through every word spoken in the Scriptures. Once the garden gate has been opened, perhaps you can wander more freely and taste all the fruits held out to you in this book of God's word. It will take a lifetime—but what a beautiful lifetime it will be.

Make this book your own. You and God together will find out what place it takes in your life and in the life of your faith community.

Using the Meditations

- Each meditation can be read in one sitting, but ideally you will let it accompany you in the course of your daily life and help you enter into prayer.

- Each meditation focuses on one passage taken from the Christian Testament. The passages are arranged in the order in which they appear in the Bible.

- As you pray these meditations, you will need the following items:
  - *A Bible.* This book does not replace the Bible, but points toward it. If you don't already own a Bible, then choose the translation that is most appropriate for you. The texts quoted in this book are all referenced to the New Revised Standard Version, so your own Bible's texts may sound a little different. Any version you read is a translation, and it's helpful to be exposed to different versions.
  - *Time.* Since you have picked up this book, you already know that time needs to be given to God and to the word of God. This book invites you to carve out some time and gives direction on how to spend that time. You and God together, therefore, will decide how and where to set aside time for the work of this book.
  - *Space.* Choose or create a physical space in which you can work with this book. If possible find one place where you can do all fifteen meditations. Ideally this space will be comfortable and will allow you to be alone. If this is impossible, then make the space as private and as beautiful as you can—

a part of coming to God is coming into beauty. You are preparing a place for yourself and your God. In whatever way you can, reserve a place for the Bible: a special table or a portion of a table, a shelf, or a surface covered with a beautiful cloth.

- *Objects.* Particular meditations will suggest other things to bring with you into your prayer space: a pen, paper, a candle, and so on.

  Keeping a prayer journal will prove helpful as you go. This simply means having one book in which you write down some of the things that you talk over with God or some of the things that happen during your prayer time or during your daily life. At the end of the fifteen meditations, you might find it helpful to have a special prayer time in which you review the path that you have recorded in your prayer journal.
- *Commitment.* Getting to know God, the word of God, and the faith of Christianity is a joy and a privilege, but it does take effort. Make a commitment to yourself to give God this time and space.
- *Prayer.* This book suggests certain ways to pray with these Scripture passages. Don't feel limited by these suggestions. If they are helpful to you, make use of them. If they open other doors for you, so much the better.
- *Yourself.* Your presence is what God really wants!
- *Other people.* This book can be used entirely in solitude, but the book along with the Scriptures will lead you toward others. Or you may have a group of people who would like to work through this book together. If you have a spiritual director, then you will want the director to be a part of this process too.

• The book is written with the idea that you will take one meditation a week. On the first day of each week, you will need time to read and work through the entire meditation. During the next six days, try to set aside a regular prayer time, even as small as five minutes before bedtime (choose the time that's easiest for you), to read the Scripture text again and to pray with it. On the seventh and last day, you may want to take a longer time so that you can review with God all that has happened during the week.

- Each chapter is divided into five sections. This format is meant not to be restrictive but simply to give some rhythm and regularity to your praying with the Scriptures. The pattern is as follows:
  - *Opening to the word.* This section suggests ways to prepare to read the particular passage. Read through the section first, then carry it out. Many meditations include suggestions for what to bring to your prayer space or how to use the meditations in a specific way.
  - *The word of God.* This section briefly introduces you to the particular Scripture text and provides a way for you to receive the message of the passage itself.
  - *Reflections on the word.* Reflections on the gift of the biblical text are offered in this section. Receive them as the fruit of meditation upon a Christian treasure. To help you receive God's word, hold it inside and treasure it.
  - *The word in action.* Some practical ways of living with the passage during the week are provided in this section. Choose one and be faithful to it. Some are simple, some more complex. Some can be done at home or at work, others require going out or acquiring something. Whichever one you choose, assume it as a way of praying not just with words but with your life. In your daily prayer, ask for God's help with this activity. At the end of the week, in prayer, review it with God.
  - *Praying with the word.* In this section a final prayer draws on some of the themes in the reflections. If you find it helpful, pray this prayer on the first day or throughout the week. You may of course prefer to pray in your own way, instead of or in addition to using this prayer.

A Final Comment

This book is developmental. Prayer doesn't happen all at once, but we learn as we go. The more we turn to God in prayer, the more we will know what prayer is. The more we take the Scriptures into our life, the more alive the Scriptures will be for us. At the end of the fifteen meditations, you will not be in the same place as that in which you began.

When you have finished the book, take a special prayer time to put before God the whole process you have experienced. Spend time with friends of faith, or with your spiritual director if you have one, reflecting on what has happened over the course of this time with the Scriptures.

This book is only one ingredient in your whole life of faith. Let it help you to find the next one. Most important, let it remind you that the good news is, indeed, love.

Matthew 11:28-30

Easy? You Call Love Easy?

Opening to the Word

When you are comfortable in your prayer space, take a deep breath. Take another. Fill your lungs, empty them. Breathe in and out again, deeply.

Feel your hands resting quietly. Feel the surface beneath your fingertips. Your hands have been busy with this and that. They have felt and done so much. Give them rest.

Sit quietly, and take another breath. Breathe in and out fully. Feel the rhythm of your breathing, the breath of God flowing within and through you, giving you life, making your blood pulse.

Let your body relax in its place. Feel the weight of it against the chair or floor or whatever you are sitting or lying on. Does any part of your body feel tired, pained, weary, burdened? your shoulders? back? legs? neck? Concentrate a moment on the part of your body that is feeling stressed, the part of your body that is speaking most loudly. Feel its pain for a moment as you sit quietly in your place. Let go of the stress.

The Word of God

Pick up your Bible, hold it in your hands, and bear this word of God for a moment. You might even close your eyes and feel its surface with your fingertips.

Now, read aloud the good news of love from the Gospel of Matthew, chapter 11, verses 28–30. Read the passage slowly. Pause and reread a sentence or phrase if you feel so moved.

Reflections on the Word

I remember a story that haunted me when I was a child. A friend of my family's had a baby boy—her first child. She and her husband were thrilled, and they cherished the baby. His name was John.

One day when John was on the verge of walking, his father entered the baby's room to take him from his crib. Reaching down he saw with horror that the baby's face was blue. John was not breathing. As a physician John's father knew what to do and soon was able to get the breath flowing again in the boy's body. But John had been without oxygen for a long time. The young parents had attached the baby's pacifier to his clothing with a string, and the string had become wound around the child's neck until he couldn't breathe.

His parents soon learned that John would never develop mentally, never learn to talk or write or even to walk. For the rest of his life, he would lie helpless and speechless.

As he became a young man physically, John remained totally dependent upon his parents. They carried the burden not only of his illness but also of feeling that his condition was due to their carelessness. Sometimes John's father wished that he had walked into the room just a few moments later, too late to save the boy's life—for what life did John have? Then John's father would feel guilty for the wish because he loved the boy, and it was his love that felt the pain. The parents were fortunate because they carried the burden together, and it drew them closer. Still, the burden bowed their shoulders.

I remember feeling, as a child, the weight of that boy's helpless life, of John's parents' constant burden of potential unfulfilled, mistakes made, love mixed with guilt and regret. It was too big a burden for me.

Their story, their pain, though uncommon in its details, is universal in its nature. No one of us is untouched by suffering, regret, guilt, or mistakes that can't be put right. The pain of

John's parents puts them in the midst of the whole human family, for we recognize and touch one another in our broken places.

In our pain—big or small, new or old—we can touch and be touched. There, we are close to the heart. For there we are close to Jesus. There, his word is for us: "'Come to me, all you that are weary and are carrying heavy burdens.'"

Jesus doesn't tell us to fix ourselves up, repair those mistakes, get rid of those burdens, and then come and see him. He wants us just as we are, burdens and all. He wants to give us comfort. He wants to embrace us. He wants to be with us in our pain.

Can we come to Jesus with the burden we carry? Can we come and lay our burden on his shoulders, our mistakes and guilt at his feet, and let him care for us? "'Come to me, . . . I will give you rest.'" This is Jesus, looking at us with love and wanting to be with us. This is the good news. Weary and heavy-laden though we may be, "'Come to me,'" our God says to us. Come.

When John was in his twenties, his parents took him to Lourdes for healing. They had never realized that in order to get to the healing waters, they would have to maneuver through a crowd of sick and suffering people. They went looking for help with their pain, but they found more pain than they had ever seen before.

To come to Jesus is to come among the weary and the heavy-laden, the sick and the afflicted. We can't come to Jesus and ignore human pain, our own or anyone else's. In Matthew's Gospel, Jesus warns his disciples three times that their walk with him will lead to the cross, but he teaches them a new way. The Sermon on the Mount in chapter 5 begins with this same word of comfort for those who are burdened. Jesus surrounds himself not with the comfortable but with the mournful, the hungry, and the poor in spirit. Here, in chapter 11, Matthew shows us Jesus calling them to be with him. At the end of his Gospel, Matthew gives us Jesus' promise that he will be with us always, wherever we are.

"'My yoke is easy, and my burden is light.'" Easy? Jesus calls love easy? How can he ask us to come into pain, our own or anyone else's, and tell us that love is easy?

Perhaps the answer is in the yoke. A yoke is a harness, a way to tie animals so that they stay together while they are working. It joins them together and makes them a team. To be joined, linked, united—that is being yoked.

"Take my yoke" is Jesus' offer to join us to him, to make him and us a team, so that our burden becomes his burden too. John's parents took him to Lourdes because they believed in God and wanted to ask for God's help. They laid their burden in God's hands. They were bound to John in both pain and love. John did not come back cured of his illness, but his parents came back healed of their burden, their guilt and regret. "'Come to me, . . . and I will give you rest.'"

The Word in Action

• Give particular attention to that sore spot in your body that you brought before God at the beginning of this meditation. During the week take care of that part of your body, be attentive to its pain, and allow God's healing to come to you there.

• Write on a sheet of paper or in your memo book, in your date book, or on your wall calendar these words of Jesus': "'Come to me, . . . and I will give you rest.'" Keep these words in sight, and repeat them aloud or silently whenever they catch your eye.

• This week be prepared for the moment when you make a mistake or feel guilt or regret for something. When that moment comes, repeat or even write down these same words of Jesus': "'Come to me, . . . and I will give you rest.'"

• Be watchful for the pain of a stranger, however small it may be. When you perceive that a person bears a burden, pray for her or him, even just for a moment. If you can give comfort to another, try to do so.

• Be alert this week for gentleness. When you sense gentleness in something or someone, or in yourself, pause. Be aware of what it feels like. Ask Jesus to teach you what gentleness means and how to be gentle.

- Notice one way in which you are “yoked,” or tied by love, to a person, a place, or perhaps a work. Give thanks to God for that bond of love and for the fidelity that allows you to bear it in love.

Praying with the Word

My God, you have called me to yourself. I come with my pains and burdens, but I come. You carry them for me, and I carry them with you. Heal the places in me that are sore and suffering. Teach me to be gentle. Ease the burdens of all who are weary, pained, or heavy-laden. Help us to enter into your rest. Thank you. Amen.

Mark 2:1–12

Faith Makes an Opening

Opening to the Word

If possible, close the doors and windows and the drapes or blinds in your prayer space. Sit in the center of the room. For five minutes concentrate on sitting as still as you can. You might even set a timer to go off after five minutes.

During these five minutes, focus your attention on remaining motionless: feet, fingertips, elbows, eyelids—every part of your body.

When the five minutes are up, relax your body completely. Move around, stretch, open the blinds and windows, allow the air back into the room.

The Word of God

Hold your Bible in your hands. Then open it to the title page and read the name it has been given. This is the Holy Bible, the Scriptures, the word of God. It is a collection of books *(biblia)* or writings *(scriptura)* that speak God to us.

Mark's is a dramatic Gospel, short but full of detail. Mark prefers to show us what Jesus does. Much of the good news in Mark about Jesus' love comes through stories of healing. One powerful passage from Mark's Gospel shows Jesus healing a paralyzed man. Slowly and attentively read aloud Mark 2:1–12.

Reflections on the Word

You can nearly always tell where a celebrity or a special person is because that person will be surrounded by a crowd. Mark shows us a crowd so large that it has filled a house. People seem to be breathing down one another's necks. They have come to see Jesus, but they have found themselves packed together. Nobody can get in or out.

This is only the second chapter of Mark's Gospel, but already we have been plunged into activity. Jesus has been traveling about Galilee healing people. Now that he has returned to their town, the people of Capernaum have come in such great numbers that the place is crammed. Besides the curious, the crowd includes many who bring pains of all kinds. They are so intent on finding relief from suffering that they prevent others from getting to Jesus.

How easy it is to get in the way of someone else's healing. How easy it is, when we are focused on our own problems, to ignore others' pain.

In this meditation's opening experience on being motionless, we realize how difficult it is to remain perfectly still. The one who is arriving in the midst of this crowd in Mark's Gospel is always still, for he is incapable of moving. He must rely on others to bring him to Jesus, to the one who may be able to heal him.

Four people have taken the paralyzed man up. Mark tells us nothing about these four friends, but they show us what it means to care for other people, what it means to be Christian. They know their friend's need for healing. They not only bring him to where Jesus is but they go to great lengths to maneuver their friend close to Jesus.

Imagine the crowd of broken, motionless people jamming up against the entrance to the house and listening to Jesus' words, seeing a shaft of daylight pierce the earthen roof, then watching the mat with the paralyzed man being lowered into the packed room. The impenetrable is penetrated because of the faith and love of those four people who wanted their friend to be healed.

Jesus turns immediately to the paralyzed man and says, "'Your sins are forgiven.'" He knows that the first thing the man needs is not to be physically healed but to be loved. Some of the people there are upset and "questioning in their hearts." Hearing someone talking about broken insides and speaking words of love tends to make us uncomfortable. But when Jesus is present, love and forgiveness are present. He gives these to the paralyzed man. He also heals the man's physical pain, for he knows that our bodies too need healing. Jesus sends the man home.

The formerly paralyzed man walks right through the crowd, and perhaps the greatest miracle in this wondrous story is that the crowd is "amazed and glorifie[s] God." Rather than being jealous because someone else is healed or angry because someone jumped queue or annoyed because Jesus' words are cut short, the crowd rejoices in another's happiness.

The paralyzed crowd is moved on this day, for faith has made an opening that has brought a person to Jesus, to healing, and to a new life. Faith makes openings for the good news of love to enter.

The Word in Action

• This week be aware of times when strangers are around you, perhaps in an elevator or in a store or on a street. Select one face that you don't know, and commit yourself to pray for that person this week.

• In your own physical environment at work, at home, or in a place where you spend a lot of time, change one physical thing, big or small. Move something. Don't put anything else in its place, just leave the spot blank for this week. At the end of the week, put in that blank place one new thing, something beautiful or pleasant, something you like to look at. Do this to remind yourself that faith makes a place for goodness to grow and to be seen.

• This week pay particular attention to requests for help, even subtle requests, from other people. Respond generously.

• Ask someone to help you with something you usually do yourself, but in reality you could use help with. Thank them for their help. Pray for them. If you like, tell them you will pray for them.

• Watch for one kind or selfless act, any occasion of someone doing something for someone else, no matter how insignificant the act may seem. If possible, let that person know you are aware that he or she did a kind thing.

• Ponder this question throughout the week: Where do I need faith to make an opening for love to grow? Write down any answers. Then, at the end of the week, try out ways of making the openings.

• Write these words on the back of a business card or any small card: "Your sins are forgiven." Keep the card with you during the week. You might take it out from time to time and read what it says, aloud or silently. At the end of the week, hold the card in your hand while you say a short prayer, aloud or silently. Pray either a known prayer, such as the Lord's Prayer, or a prayer of your own. Then tear or cut up the card and throw it out.

Praying with the Word

God, you have promised to be with me. Help me to find you at the center of every crowd of people. Help me to find you in the center of my own life. Help me to open doors, windows, and even roofs for those who need you. Bring comfort and peace where there is pain. Give me compassion for those who suffer and joy for those who rejoice. Grace me with faith to make openings to love. Move my heart to praise and thank you always, for you are my life. Amen. Alleluia.

Luke 9:43–51

Let This Sink In

Opening to the Word

In your prayer place, find a bare spot on one of the walls. Stand with your back against the wall, body pressed up against it, leaning on it. Feel the support of the wall on your legs, your back, your shoulders, your head. Stand there a moment, as straight as you can.

Now, still standing against the wall, reach out with your arms as far as they will go, stretching right to your fingertips. Reach up and all around, extending your arms into the air, moving them in the space around you. While remaining firmly fixed at the wall, stretch your arms as much as possible.

Then, step away from the wall so that you can move freely behind you as well as in front of you. Give your whole body a good stretch.

Take a moment to give thanks to God for the things in your life that give you firm support and for the things in your life that allow you to move freely, to stretch.

The Word of God

Hold your Bible in your hands. Give thanks for the word of God that you are now holding and that is a gift to you.

Open the Bible and find the beginning and the end of the Christian Testament. Read the first verse, Matthew 1:1, and the last two verses, Revelation 22:20–21.

The pages of the Christian Testament hold the Good News of Jesus Christ, who is here and who is coming. Leaf through these pages. As you turn the pages, you learn of God's love. As your life unfolds, you are telling of God's love.

Now turn to the Gospel of Luke. Read aloud chapter 9, verses 43–51. Remember to take your time. If you want to read all or parts of this passage several times, do so. Attend to these words as you would to the words of a beloved.

Reflections on the Word

When I was growing up, I loved studying constellations, planets, asteroids, comets—the mysteries of space. Whenever I had the chance, I visited the museums where I could see Apollo rockets, space shuttles, lunar modules, satellites, and other such marvels.

But the single most dramatic item that I found in these museums was one of a different nature. In a darkened room, I came across a life-size display of the gray, dusty lunar landscape, footprints and all, silent and still. Standing on it with its back to me was a figure wearing the lunar space suit. All around was darkness. Far away glowed the luminous disk of the earth, on which the tiny continents and oceans could clearly be seen. I looked over the astronaut's shoulder toward my distant home. All around was more emptiness, more distance, more unknown, and more darkness. In the immeasurable vastness of the universe, this astronaut stood so tiny.

Like the astronaut on the moon looking back at the earth, we can look back over where we have come from to help us see our true place in the universe. God shows us who we are, if we pay attention. What may seem to be random events are really the loving presence of God calling us forth.

The journey of the disciples is a journey of both love and suffering. In chapter 5 of Luke's Gospel, these men are fishing. Jesus calls them from their daily task, from a place they understand. They turn to go with him. In that one simple and undramatic moment, everything changes. Like the man on the moon's, it is a small step but a giant one.

One step at a time, the disciples follow Jesus. They walk with him into crowds and into lonely places, into successes and into failures, into pain and into joy. The pace of activity in chapters 4 through 9 of Luke is breathtaking. Healings come one after the other. Through it all, the disciples are learning who Jesus is and who they are as they walk with him, learning about love.

By the end of Luke, chapter 9, this walk with Jesus takes the disciples, apparently, to success. Luke tells us that everybody is amazed at all that Jesus is doing. But, this moment of success is the very moment that Jesus chooses to remind them that he is going to be betrayed. In the midst of success, Jesus speaks of failure. In the midst of new life, he speaks of death. In the midst of greatness, he speaks of lowliness. No wonder they "[do] not understand."

Like the astronaut on the moon, the disciples' step away from home has shown them that they are at the edge of a vast, unknown universe. Now is the moment when they can choose, either to stand gazing back at the home they have left or to turn and face the new, unknown life.

In confusion the disciples begin to quarrel among themselves. Which of them is greatest? They quarrel with a stranger, demanding to know who he is to be talking about Jesus. They are being called to step away from the firm support of the wall, to stretch and move freely. By reminding the disciples that he will be betrayed, Jesus asks the disciples to take the next step with him and find out where it goes.

Now he "set[s] his face to go to Jerusalem." This verse (9:51) is a turning point in Luke's Gospel. Over the next ten chapters, Jesus journeys steadily toward Jerusalem; toward the center of faith; toward the place where he will be betrayed, suffer, and die, toward the place where he will be raised to new life.

Afraid, confused, hesitant, the disciples turn and walk with Jesus, not knowing where he leads. They don't know where they are going, but they do know the One who invites them.

Perhaps love is not so much arriving somewhere as going somewhere. We have a personal invitation from the One who wants to travel with us. If we, like the disciples, have felt the longing, the fear, and the desire; if we have reached to the moon and glimpsed the expanse of creation; if we have been moved by love of Jesus to go wherever he will lead us, trusting in this good news of love; then we have entered into God's way.

The Word in Action

• Do you recall in your own life a step you took, a moment when you went somewhere you wouldn't usually go, the kind of small step that made all the difference? Look back at your story, and rediscover these steps. Then, in a thanksgiving litany, give thanks to God for these steps, or ask forgiveness for steps that took you away from love.

• Begin something, any small thing that you have been meaning to do: a book you have intended to read, a room you have wanted to paint, a letter you have needed to write. Begin it, and ask God to be with you in the task. Read and ponder Luke 9:51 again: "When the days drew near for him to be taken up, he set his face to go to Jerusalem."

• When someone else is confused about something, make a point of trying to help that person come to understanding. Be patient, remembering Jesus' words about welcoming the child.

• The disciples were displeased when they saw someone else casting out demons in Jesus' name. Ponder Jesus' response in Luke 9:50: "'Do not stop him; for whoever is not against you is for you.'" Consider some people who may be outside your congregation or religion but who do good for the human family. If you can, thank them or help them in some way. At the least ask God to bless their good work.

• Take a walk by yourself without first planning where you will go. For a set length of time (fifteen minutes, half an hour, an hour), let your feet direct you. Bring with you this Scripture passage from Luke, and read it sometime during your walk. Ponder that each footstep taken in love, each moment of loving, brings us closer to the new Jerusalem, the Reign of God.

• Talk to one person you know who is a person of faith. Tell him or her about things that Jesus has done in your life, in another's life, and in the Scriptures. Ask that person to tell you three things. If you don't know a person you can talk to this way, then write down three things and send or give them to someone.

Praying with the Word

Dear God, you have walked for us a path of lowliness, suffering, service, and above all love. Let me journey with you. When I am afraid, give me courage. When I am confused, give me understanding. When I am lost, stay with me. Bring me to the new life you have promised. Thank you for all the good things you have given me and for all the difficult things that have helped me to grow. May your word continue to grow in me, so that I may speak it to others. May I always remember that your good news is love. Amen.

John 1:35–51

Come and Get It

Opening to the Word

Place your Bible in a special place in your prayer space. Then put something of special meaning to you or something of beauty near the word of God.

Stand with your back toward the place where your Bible sits. Stand there quietly a few moments and look around. Observe all that is before you, the familiar and the unfamiliar, the big and the small, the important and the unimportant. Take it in.

After a few moments, turn around so that you are facing in the opposite direction. Stand in this new view for a few moments more, again observing everything in front of you.

Now, close your eyes and recall all that you saw in the room. In the presence of God's word, ask God to open your heart to all that is around you.

The Word of God

Open your Bible to the beginning of the Christian Testament. Read aloud the first verse of the first Gospel, Matthew 1:1.

Turn to the second Gospel, Mark, and read aloud the first sentence. Then turn to the third Gospel and read its first sentence, Luke 1:1–4.

Finally, turn to the beginning of the fourth Gospel and read out loud the first sentence there: "In the beginning was the Word, and the Word was with God, and the Word was God."

Now, let the word of God be spoken to you. Turn to today's Scripture passage, John 1:35–51, and read it, preferably aloud.

After you have read it, pause a few moments and sit quietly. You don't need to think about anything. Don't worry about trying to concentrate on the passage. Just sit with it, and let it sit with you.

Reflections on the Word

When was the last time you had a chance to be by yourself and do nothing in particular? Perhaps you stayed at home in front of the television. Perhaps you went shopping. Perhaps you went outdoors, sat under a tree with a book or a snack, and dreamed. In just such a moment, we meet Nathanael. John's Gospel does not tell us much about who Nathanael is. We meet him sitting under a fig tree, waiting.

Suddenly, into this ordinary moment, while the fig tree is quietly growing, bursts an excited person with an unbelievable announcement: "'We have found the Messiah.'" No matter how expected it may be, the arrival of someone or something always seems to take us by surprise. We wait for births, we wait for deaths, but even the most predicted ones make us catch our breath.

Philip, a friend of Nathanael's, arrives in the middle of this quiet, ordinary day to tell his friend that the time has come. But this news of a promise fulfilled comes with a catch ending. The Messiah, the Anointed One, the one whose coming would signify that all God's promises to Israel were being fulfilled, turns out to be from nowhere—Nazareth. "'Can anything good come out of Nazareth?'" asks Nathanael.

Can God's promise be brought about through regular people, no more or less handsome than anyone else, with names and histories and family ties? Doesn't God work in the wondrous, the mysterious, the miraculous, the glorious?

Nathanael is faced with a decision. Should he listen to his friend's joyful, crazy news, rouse himself, and risk being disappointed? Or should he go back under his tree and wait for something dramatic, foolproof, and unmistakable?

As this story and many other biblical stories testify, God does not speak only in the big, bold events. God speaks in our life, in every moment, and in every possible way. God comes right into our life: where we are doing the dishes, where we are struggling to get to work on time. This is where God comes—where we are.

The good news of Jesus' coming is that the God of love need not be sought "out there." God has camped among us and come to live with us. The one we long for has arrived in our midst. The life we seek is here. Wherever we are, we are not removed from God.

When Nathanael chooses to get up from his comfortable spot, when he answers Philip's invitation to "'come and see,'" he finds that the one he is seeking already knows him. Before he even gets to Jesus, Jesus calls him by name.

"'I saw you under the fig tree,'" Jesus tells the astonished Nathanael, "'before Philip called you.'" Nathanael found Jesus because Jesus was looking for him, and his friend Philip helped him to see. Having come this far, Nathanael is able to say something much bigger than he knows, much truer than he can yet understand: "'You are the son of God!'" he tells Jesus. "'You are the King of Israel!'" is a statement that comes out of Nathanael's whole history, both his own life and the life of his people. Because he knows the Promise, he can recognize it when it comes, even if it comes at a time and in a way that he did not expect. He recognizes it in Jesus.

This moment of insight will unfold for Nathanael in the days to come, for it is in the events of our own life that we learn who God is. Nathanael will learn only in his travels with Jesus.

And Jesus tells Nathanael that if he comes and sees, he "'will see greater things'": the glory of heaven spilling over into earth. Jesus' presence shows that God is here in our world, exactly where we are, as close as our own flesh and blood. We don't have to escape our life to see God's glory. God's glory comes to us. Like Nathanael, to discover the good news of love, we must only "'come and see.'"

The Word in Action

• Find one instance in your life when a dream became a reality. Tell someone the story of this dream and how it came about and what part it has in your life now. Then, ponder your response to this question: How do I keep the Promise of Christ alive in my heart and in my actions?

• This week, if you meet someone you've never met before, say the person's name out loud and pray for her or him. Try to look at this person as Jesus looked at Nathanael, that is, seeing her or him as a child of God, a sister or a brother. How will you invite this person to travel with you?

• In your home pick out the most familiar, well known, and ordinary object you can find, perhaps something you've had for years. Put a giant red bow or a flower or a bright yellow sticker on it. Whenever it catches your eye, give thanks to God for it and for all ordinary, familiar things, saying, "Yes, God, our creator, this is good."

• Go someplace you don't usually go. It could be to a street you've never set foot on, a chair you don't generally sit in, a corner store you've always passed by, a child's swing in a public playground, or a hidden stream or brook. Give yourself at least ten minutes there. Afterward, write down or draw everything you saw while you were there. Then, talk to God about inner or outer places that Christ might want you to come and see in the future.

• Write down Nathanael's statement to Jesus, "'You are the Son of God!'" Keep with you the sheet on which this is written. In a moment of prayer to God, begin with the words, "You are," and finish them in your own way.

Praying with the Word

Thank you, God, for the places you have put me, for the things you have given me, for all that is familiar and comfortable in my life. Help me to see your presence in all these things. In times of waiting, give me patience. In times of change, give me courage. In times of fulfillment, give me a grateful heart. Give me boldness to speak your word to others and openness to hear your word that others speak to me, that I may learn to see your glory. For you are my God. Amen.

Acts of the Apostles 5:40–42

Cause for Rejoicing

Opening to the Word

As usual place your Bible in its special place and your seat next to it. Put a new candle and some matches beside the Bible. Sitting before God's holy word, acknowledge the presence of the Holy Spirit with you at this moment. Invite the Spirit to fill your mind and heart and body.

Now, in the presence of the Spirit, recall a time in your life when you felt beaten or when you had failed at something. Did you feel that you had no way out of the situation? Did you feel that nothing you could do would make it better?

Bring this moment to the Spirit of wisdom and truth, and ask the Spirit to heal and help you in it.

The Word of God

Open the Bible to the last page of the Gospel of Luke. Read the final four verses (24:50–53).

Now, turn to the beginning of the Acts of the Apostles. Read Acts 1:1–2.

Luke and Acts were probably written by the same author. Acts continues the story begun in the Gospel of Luke. Beginning with Pentecost, Acts tells the story of the earliest days of the church. It describes how the Good News spread from Jerusalem to Rome. Acts spins the story of the spirit of God at work in the life of ordinary people.

Now, turn to today's passage, Acts 5:40–42, and read it aloud once. Then, light the candle.

Reflections on the Word

One evening I listened to a beaten man. Robert was about forty years old, with graying hair and a friendly smile tinged with pain. Although he was soft-spoken, once he started talking, his story poured out.

Three years before he had had a house in a fashionable part of town, a truck and a car, a wife and a daughter and a son, a good job, and a comfortable life. He had worked hard for those things.

Now Robert was sitting in a drop-in center, surrounded by the urban poor, holding a cup of coffee, waiting for a free meal, and telling his story to a stranger.

The crash had come suddenly. He had lost his job, become addicted to cocaine, and, while he spent time in jail, a friend of his had left his own wife and children to move into Robert's house with Robert's wife and children. Of the life he had built over forty years, nothing was left.

Robert "lost it" and lost himself. By the time I met him, he had spent a couple of years on the streets, sleeping anywhere, experiencing "shutdown," out of communication with everybody. He had nothing to hope for, nothing to live for—no name, no life, no way. He was a beaten man.

The Apostles, in today's passage from Acts, seem to be beaten men too. They have been imprisoned by the leaders of their own people. They own nothing, have no livelihood, and live nowhere. They appear to have no future.

Since Jesus' Crucifixion and Resurrection, the Apostles have led a precarious existence in Jerusalem. However, at Pentecost, the Holy Spirit filled them with life and joy, and now they overflow with the Good News and have been telling everyone about it. Large crowds have listened to them proclaiming publicly what they were once afraid to whisper secretly: that Jesus of Nazareth is the Anointed One of God, that God loves us totally and faithfully, that death is conquered, and that there is a new way.

In the first five chapters of Acts, Luke describes how dramatically the Apostles' lives have been changing. According to the narrative, less than two months after Jesus' death and Resurrection, these friends who had run away from the horror of Jesus' execution are now telling a crowd of several thousand that Jesus has been raised to life by God and is the Christ, the one sent to free the people.

Peter and the Apostles are uneducated, rough people, but they boldly speak dangerous words that are being taken to heart by people around them. In the name of Jesus, they have been doing so much good that people "carried out the sick into the streets, and laid them on cots and mats, in order that Peter's shadow might fall on some of them as he came by" (Acts 5:15).

Peter and John had been arrested, reprimanded, and released (Acts 4). They spoke more boldly still. As a result, they were again imprisoned (Acts 5). The leaders of those who had not accepted Christ "were enraged and wanted to kill them" (v. 33). The Apostles have been forbidden, at the price of death, to do precisely what they believe God has asked them to do: to speak the name that gives them joy, to do the work that gives meaning to their life.

The Apostles' response to the threats is quite different from what it once would have been. They know now that the presence of pain does not erase the much deeper presence of God. This does not mean that they like to suffer, or that pain is God's will for them, but they know that they have found a treasure in the name of Jesus Christ. Forbidden to speak the name of Jesus, flogged and threatened with death, they go out rejoicing. Even hatred does not prevent them from speaking God's word. This must bewilder their opponents. After all, how can an enemy that takes strength from suffering and power from weakness ever be defeated?

When we are most in control, most secure, most competent, it can be hard to admit that our lasting strength comes from Jesus. Robert, in the story that opened this reflection, discovered this by losing everything. The night I spoke with him, he told me that he had been writing out a thank-you list. "I have more to be thankful for now than I have ever had in my life," he said. "I know now what real friends are, the friends who met me on the street. I lost all I had, but what I have now can never be taken away from me. There's no place I can go that God won't be. I know because when I had nothing else and no place else to turn, God was there."

Robert still lives in a rooming house, still longs for his wife and children, still does not understand what happened, and still does not know the next step. But out of his suffering, as with the Apostles, has come a grateful heart, a heart that knows that the good news is love, even for—maybe especially for—the lowly.

The Word in Action

• Recall one person who is no longer part of your life. If possible get out a picture of that person. This week pray for the person, and put into God's hands all that you have lost in losing that person. If reconciliation is possible, seek it.

• Sit down and, as quickly as you can, write out on some nice paper a list of things for which you are thankful. Put the list in your Bible at Acts, chapter 5.

• Write down one thing that you believe about God. Show or speak this belief to one person during the week.

• Is there something you have been afraid to do? This could be anything: learning to parallel park, forgiving someone who has hurt you, visiting someone in a nursing home. Pray for God's help with this one thing. Ask that God's love might drive out fear. Then do what you have been afraid to do.

• Choose one thing to which you are very attached: your watch, your best jacket, a favorite houseplant, your morning newspaper, a special treat that you have been saving. Ponder again today's verses from Acts, which show the freedom from fear and the detachment from things that the Apostles felt. Then, either give this thing away and don't replace it for a week, if at all, or buy its equivalent and give that away.

• This week when you pray, say aloud the words for which the Apostles were flogged: "Jesus is the Christ." Speak to one Christian you know, ask what he or she thinks these words mean, and talk about what you think they mean.

Praying with the Word

Dear God, you gave us Jesus to be our companion and our guide. Forgive me for the times I have deserted him or been afraid to proclaim his name. Show me how to fill my life with your love and to speak your word of truth wherever I can. Grant that, when sorrow or distress comes my way, I may remember to call upon you for help and to rejoice in your abundant love. I thank you for all that you have given me, and I commit it to your keeping. Amen. Alleluia.

Acts of the Apostles 9:1–19

Breathing Fire

Opening to the Word

Retire to your place of prayer. On a piece of paper, write down the name of someone you love or have loved, or someone who has had a unique place in your life. Put this piece of paper on the place reserved for your Bible, and put the Bible on top of it.

Call to mind a time when you have felt quite alone and isolated. Did you feel deserted or abandoned? Did it seem impossible to talk to anyone or to let anyone in? Did you long to touch or be touched by someone? Linger in these remembrances of loneliness.

In the stillness of your heart, ask God to come in. Ask God to touch this place where no one else has been. Ask God to fill your emptiness. Take a moment to pray for the person on whose name your Bible rests.

The Word of God

Turn to the Acts of the Apostles again. Glance through the first chapter or two, and read aloud all the personal names you find there.

Acts is filled with people: the very first members of the church, the Apostles, and their friends. This book is about their acts, the things they did, not by themselves but through the power of the Holy Spirit. The Spirit is the real actor in this drama. But the Spirit acts with and through Peter, Mary, John, Stephen, Tabitha, Philip, Priscilla, Barnabas, Timothy, Paul, and many others whose names we do not know.

Before you read today's passage, pray that these earliest Christians might help you to feel the presence of that same spirit of God. Now read Acts 9:1–19.

Reflections on the Word

We know little about him beyond his name: Ananias. He lives in Damascus and belongs to the local community of the Way of Jesus, which has been creating commotion in his region. Since Pentecost the Christians have disturbed devout Jews, the Romans, and just about everyone by proclaiming publicly that Jesus is the Christ, the Anointed One of God.

On the one hand, people bring their sick to the Apostles in the hope that at least Peter's shadow might touch them, and the number of disciples has increased greatly in Jerusalem. But on the other hand, the more the disciples speak the Good News, the more opposition is aroused. Throughout the first eight chapters of Acts, the tension has been increasing rapidly.

When Stephen speaks the Good News, his listeners cover their ears, rush against him, and stone him to death. They lay their coats at the feet of a young man named Saul, who completely approves of the killing.

Saul is a man of fire and devotion. Not long after Stephen's death, he obtains official letters authorizing him to arrest anyone who invokes the name of Jesus. He sets out for Damascus to capture any followers of the Way that he finds there.

Meanwhile, in Damascus, Ananias hears his name called. He knows who is calling him, and he readily replies, "'Here I am.'" Even so he is not quite prepared for the task that God gives him: to go to Saul and lay hands on him. Aghast, Ananias explains, "'I have heard from many about this man, how much evil he has done to your saints in Jerusalem.'" Surely if God knew the situation, God would not ask such a thing.

God's requests often come in strange forms. Generally, they seem to come at the wrong time, in the wrong way, and to the wrong person. Ananias, a man of faith, takes exception to God's request, which must seem foolish, dangerous, and pointless to him. In response God gives no guarantees or explanations, and he says that Ananias must go. Ananias goes.

When Ananias sees Saul, he greets him as "'Brother Saul,'" not as an enemy but as family. Ananias stakes his life on God's unlikely story that Saul belongs to Christ. Then, Ananias pronounces the name that Saul is fighting against: "'Jesus . . . has sent me.'" Ananias goes with fear and trembling, but also with love and faith, believing that he is in the presence and power of the spirit of God.

Saul had set out for Damascus in power and authority. He arrived blind and broken. He waits to understand the flash of lightning and the voice on the road. This educated, determined man who has known and served God all his life has encountered the Christ: "'I am Jesus, whom you are persecuting.'" The light blinded Saul. Now he waits for his eyes to be opened.

God acts in Saul's life—and in our life—in ways that touch us where we can be reached. With his fiery spirit and staunch convictions, Saul would not be turned around. Yet God stops him. Saul, who was so sure of God, now asks, "'Who are you?'" Saul, who saw things so clearly, cannot see anything now. Saul, who walked with such determination, has to be led by the hand. He waits in darkness.

But into this darkness come hands and a voice. The God who loves all of us sends Ananias. Saul hears an unknown voice speak his name and the name of Jesus. He feels hands laid upon him, not in anger or hostility but in tenderness and strength. Into Saul's darkness comes light, true sight. Into his emptiness comes fullness, the fullness of the Holy Spirit. In his place of loneliness and darkness, Saul finds a companion of the Way. Immediately, he sees. He is baptized. He regains his strength. And he gains a new name, Paul.

God's word to each of us is not always a comfortable word, is seldom predictable, and is not easily understood or lived. But it is a word of healing. It brings more than we can ask for or even imagine, as Saul himself later wrote. It leads not to isolation and loneliness but to communion.

The Word in Action

• Tell someone or write about your first name: where you got it, how you feel about it, what you know about it. Thank God for the name you have been given and for the name by which you are called.

• Take the person's name that you placed under your Bible at the beginning of this meditation. Do something loving for that person in whatever way you can, whether she or he is dead or living. Tell that person or someone else how she or he has called you into fuller life. Pray for this Ananias in your life.

• Reach out to someone in love, as Ananias does to Paul. Provide some service for a person who is alone or lonely, someone you know personally or someone in an isolated situation. For instance, call a local nursing home and ask the staff about a patient who would like to receive a letter or a visit.

• Paul brought all the passion that had been directed against the Christians to preaching the Good News. God knocked him to the ground to get his attention, but God certainly did not want to strip Paul of his passion. God calls us to use our unique character and gifts to be the good news. Talk with God about passion and about the unique gifts that you are given to spread the good news of love.

• Ask God to show you ways in which you are blind to God's grace and call in your life. Begin by lighting a candle and inviting the Spirit to enlighten you and by praying slowly and repeatedly, "Come, spirit of God, with your light for my soul." Ask for the light to see God's grace and call and also for direction about how to respond in action.

• Try to get in touch with someone who has disappeared from your life or whom you haven't seen for a while or with whom you have lost contact. If you can't find the person, write in a letter what you would like to say in person, and keep the letter in your Bible.

Praying with the Word

Dear Jesus, thank you for giving me your name to speak. Thank you for the name by which you have called me to your side. When I am in the dark, come with your light and help me to see clearly. When I am alone, be with me. Help me to receive those whom you send to me and to care for those whom you give me to love. Help especially those who are burdened by loneliness and isolation. Teach us to love one another. Amen. Alleluia.

Acts of the Apostles 23:1–11

Courage

Opening to the Word

Before entering your prayer space, put on clothes that you feel comfortable and at ease in. Put your Bible in its special place. Sit comfortably. Let your body relax. Breathe deeply.

With your hand, feel your heartbeat on your wrist, on your neck, or over your heart. Close your eyes and feel against your skin the warmth of your blood, the pulse of life within you, the rhythm of your heart.

Ask God for openness to the presence of the Spirit dwelling within you—deep, constant, hidden, inescapable—offering life.

The Word of God

Open your Bible to the Acts of the Apostles. Ponder that you hold here the life of the early church, the Spirit at work in the Body of Christ.

Turn again to the opening verses of Acts, chapter 1. Keeping one hand there, turn to the end of the Book of Acts and put your other hand there. At the beginning Jesus is taken up from his disciples, and so their eyes are turned heavenward. At the end the converted Paul is waiting under house arrest in Rome, but teaching boldly about Jesus.

Within these pages Christ has not departed at all, but lives on in the community of believers. They make him known by who they are and what they do, in their own places and in their own circumstances.

Turn now to chapter 23 and read verses 1–11.

Reflections on the Word

In the Acts of the Apostles, Paul becomes an increasingly dominant figure, traveling to many places, getting to know and be known by other Christians, establishing and strengthening churches in many cities. But in telling the story, the author of Acts is not simply describing the actions of a famous individual as though he were writing the biography of a rock star or a war hero. Rather, he is showing how the Spirit works in the heart of Paul and of his companions. Acts is a book of the heart, of the Spirit, and of the church.

Paul's task brings him pain and confusion, joy and friendship, unexpected afflictions, and unlooked-for assistance. We see him beaten, praised, denounced as a blasphemer, worshiped as a god, thrown into prison, and smuggled out of dangerous places. He finds close friends, such as Timothy and Silas, and also parts painfully from companions, as in his quarrels with John, Mark, and Barnabas. At all times Paul lives out the words the Lord spoke about him to Ananias in chapter 9 of Acts: "'I . . . will show him how much he must suffer for the sake of my name'" (v. 16).

By the time described in chapter 23, Paul is notorious. Trouble seems to follow wherever he goes. He tends to provoke people. Yet he is determined to come to Jerusalem, the most volatile place of all, despite the forebodings of his own people who are sure he will be in danger there. Having arrived, he has aroused such hostility that the Roman authorities have taken him into custody, mainly to keep him from being killed. The Roman commander has put him in the midst of a council of his own leaders. Previously, the priests, Pharisees, and Sadducees admired Paul's zeal. Today, he stands before them as a prisoner, a rebel, a blasphemer. They strike him in the mouth for his first words to them. This is the situation to which his conversion has led him.

Like Paul, we may find trouble, chaos, and confusion of one kind or another even when we think that we are listening to God. Sometimes it seems as though our own mistakes are our downfall. Sometimes it seems that God just doesn't come through for us.

Yet the words for which Paul is struck are words of faith: "'I have lived my life with a clear conscience before God.'" At this critical moment, he blames neither God nor himself. He does not give up on his mission or decide to try again another day when things are less complicated. He doesn't try to smooth things over. Instead, he speaks a word of faith. Patient waiting, trust in God's timing, and faith despite adverse circumstances—these are Paul's weapons.

Knowing the leaders to be divided, Paul uses their internal discord against them. "'I am on trial concerning the hope of the resurrection of the dead,'" he declares, knowing that this remark will stir up a long-standing source of conflict between the two parties who make up the council. Indeed, their anger turns away from him and toward each other. The factions start to quarrel among themselves, and so they are unable to harm him. Instead of running away from the storm and violence, Paul uses its power against it.

Paul's patient faith reminds me of a child who used to come with her parents to have dinner with us at our drop-in center on Wednesday nights. Three years old, Laura never spoke, never smiled, and barely looked at us when we talked to her. This family came to us every week for many months. Every time, Laura crushed plants, threw food on the floor, and, whenever possible, ran out into the street.

One Wednesday night, after an absence of a few weeks, I was working in the kitchen when I felt something touch my legs. Turning around I beheld, hugging my knees and smiling up at me, the previously remote and unresponsive Laura, now nearly five years old. I discovered for the first time that she had a charming dimple and a glow in her eyes. She held up her arms and grunted the first word I had ever heard her speak: "Up!" That grunted word was sweet music. It had taken two years for that word to come forth, and, after two years of waiting, I was privileged to hear it.

God waits patiently, much more patiently than we can begin to understand. God waits for the right moment, the moment when we will be able to hear the word of love that God longs to speak to us, the moment when we will be able to speak our own word—the moment, perhaps, that we would least expect. God loves to take us by surprise!

So it was with Paul. Just when matters looked most dire, "the Lord stood near him and said, 'Keep up your courage!'" Paul has learned to listen to such messages from God. Paul has indeed followed his Master to arrest, trial, and humiliation. Now he will go where Jesus himself never went: to Rome, the center of the Western world's power. Just as Jesus, in the Gospel of Luke, set his face toward Jerusalem, the place of trial and triumph, so Paul now is set toward Rome, where he will give witness.

The word *martyr* comes from the Greek verb meaning "witness." It has often been said that the church was founded on the blood of the martyrs. By their death as by their life, they proclaimed the name of Jesus and the power of God to bring life out of death.

We need not proclaim our faith by death in the Roman circus. Instead, our witness or martyrdom usually comes in moments of daily courage, patient love, faithful confusion, and desperate prayer. Our assurance is that God will stand near us and say, "'Keep up your courage!'" just as God stood near Paul in this story.

The Word in Action

• "'Just as you have testified for me in Jerusalem, so you must bear witness also in Rome.'" Recall one moment in your life when you said yes to God. This week be attentive for one request, however small, that God might make of you, and say, "Yes." Start each day by asking God for the grace to hear clearly when the request is made.

• This week, if you find yourself in the presence of a quarrel, fight, or disagreement, pause and ask God for peace. Then, speak the word that God gives to you or hold back the word that God asks you not to speak.

• "'I have lived my life with a clear conscience before God.'" Every night this week, before you go to bed, write down these words of Paul's, and pray them repeatedly. Ask God to clear your conscience and to make these words true in your life. If you need to ask forgiveness from someone or if you need to forgive someone or yourself, try to do so before you go to bed.

• Learn three new, useful words (you might find them in the newspaper, in a book, or just by leafing through the dictionary). Use them at every possible occasion this week, in speaking and in writing. At the end of the week, give thanks to God for the words you have been given and for your ability to speak them.

• Where is your Rome—the place or situation in which you have the most difficult time witnessing to God's love, such as a difficult relationship or an old familiar problem? Converse with God about your Rome. Ask for the grace you need to go there and give witness.

• In your life this week, whenever you catch yourself trying to escape from something, stop a moment. Instead, say (aloud, if possible) the word, "Courage."

Praying with the Word

God, you are my life. You direct my words, thoughts, and actions. Calm my fears, forgive my failings, and guide my steps. Hold me close so that I might not escape your love but instead become aware of your constant presence within me. Give me the word you would have me speak with my life. Help me to become who I am and to live what I believe. Teach me when to wait patiently, when to speak boldly, and when to listen quietly. Let my life and my death witness to the good news of your love. Amen. Alleluia.

2 Corinthians 4:1–12

Brighter and Brighter

Opening to the Word

Leave your Bible closed. Sit, stand, or kneel with your hands upraised to God. Ask God to open your heart, mind, body, and soul to the power of the word spoken in the Scriptures and in your experience.

In this position of openness, recollect a moment of failure or defeat, a time in your life when you were unable to do what you wanted to accomplish. Expose this wound, and let God come into it.

Pray from the heart about this wound, and then offer the Lord's Prayer.

The Word of God

Ponder your closed Bible. Now open the Bible, just as you opened your heart and mind to God.

Turn to the Letters, or Epistles, of Paul. Imagine the celebration of one of the early Christian communities when they received one of Paul's letters. Communication being what it was, a letter had to be a rare treat. When a community received one, copies were made and circulated among surrounding communities of Christians. They knew that their friend Paul had an important message just for them—even though sometimes the message was hard to hear.

Paul's letters predate the Acts of the Apostles and the Gospels and remind us that the Christian Testament was collected because the church needed these documents to remind them who Christ was and who they were. The community of believers came first, and out of that faith came the Scriptures.

Turn to the second letter Paul sent to the Corinthians. Paul wrote this frank letter to the people of Corinth after his relationship with them had been sorely tested. Evidently, it follows a serious quarrel between them and Paul. The Corinthians were upset at some of the things Paul wrote to them and more upset still when he canceled a planned visit to them. Recognizing how precious and how fragile the community's love was and knowing how close he was to losing it, Paul wrote this letter.

Find chapter 4 and read aloud verses 1–12.

Reflections on the Word

One day a friend of mine took me to see the taping of a popular television show. It was a late-night event. With our special tickets, we walked right past the throng of people gathered outside in the hope of seeing their TV idols. Being early we had time to look around and see what a television studio was like. Five different sets were laid out in front of us, along with several TV monitors overhead. So we could either watch the real thing or watch the screen image.

The comedy show, a series of sketches, led in the ratings. The audience was ready to laugh and applaud on cue. My friend and I were impressed with the efficiency and organization with which these masters of illusion could create a scene, then move to the next set and do it all again, while dismantling the first set and making it over into something else. We watched the actors getting into and out of makeup, having their hair and costumes straightened, and being placed in the perfect spot for sound and lighting. Now and then they would joke with the audience, but mostly they were intent on their work of making what was unreal look real.

Only God creates from nothing, but we can arrange real things to hide the truth, to make what is unreal seem real. Most of us have met people who spend their life hiding behind the image they create, keeping their true self well hidden, possibly even from themselves. A living treasure—the true self—dwells inside the carefully constructed package, but it also dwells in clay jars.

Paul tells the Corinthians, "We have this treasure." Most of us, finding ourselves in possession of a treasure, would guard it carefully. The Hope diamond, a magnificently polished marvel of clear blue purity, is thoroughly guarded inside a bulletproof case inside a sealed room inside a locked building. We don't put at risk our most precious things.

The treasure Paul talks about, the treasure that is you and God's spirit in you, is the most precious of all, but God keeps it in clay jars—common, ordinary pots and vessels meant for daily use. After all, God's way is not the human way. From God's point of view, all creation is precious, even the clay jar. The treasure inside has been given by God to be enjoyed and used in daily life and shared with all people.

Instead of locking this treasure away, the Apostles allowed the Holy Spirit to empower them to go to perilous places and share it. As Paul indicates, they had been perplexed, persecuted, and knocked down. The treasure of the good news of love is so wonderful that it cannot be contained in bulletproof boxes and sealed rooms. Spreading the good news may crack the clay jar, but, as Paul declares, "we are afflicted in every way, but not crushed." God's good news prevails.

What God has and who God is are freely ours, not because we deserve them, not because we are particularly good at taking care of them, but simply because of God's love for us. This love is handed over to us in the humblest of ways. Our own flesh and blood, our daily life, the work we do, the words we speak, the trials we undergo—these are the vessels by which God's love is borne into the world today. God chose clay jars precisely because the light of Christ will shine so much more gloriously through them. Thus, Paul asks the Corinthians to state the truth openly, letting the glory of God shine brightly.

We can create a TV set, an image of beauty and success, an illusion of happiness. We cannot create love, and we cannot create ourselves. These are God's work being done in us when we say yes to them. When effort leads to failure, when illusions shatter, we need to remember that our hidden treasure is always God's gift to us. The treasure of God's own love is stored in these fragile clay jars—in us—"so that it may be made clear that this extraordinary power belongs to God and does not come from us."

The Word in Action

• This week put away one physical thing that you use to cover up the way you really look or to hide a vulnerability. Put that physical thing in your prayer space. During the week converse with God about whether you rely too much on outward appearance and forget the wondrous treasure of God's love inside you. At the end of the week, in prayer, decide whether or not you will go back to that physical thing.

• Paul's letter was meant to heal his relationship with the Corinthians. Offer a broken relationship into God's care. Search for one step that you can take to heal this relationship. Ask for God's help in this search. Maybe, like Paul, you can start with a letter.

• Keep a treasure, such as a piece of jewelry, an awards medal, or something else of value to you in a pocket or in your purse. Whenever you think of it, hold it in your hand and ask God to remind you of the real treasure that you carry inside.

• Reflect, in prayer, on some place in your life where you have been afraid to speak the truth. In prayer seek to know the truth of this matter. Ask God to guide you in how you might speak it, whether with words or by the way you live.

• Recall the moment of failure or defeat to which you opened yourself at the beginning of this chapter. Make a card. On the inside write or draw something that represents this failure. On the outside write or illustrate these words of Saint Paul: "This extraordinary power belongs to God and does not come from us."

• In conversations you have this week, make a conscious effort not to hide behind false words. Concentrate on speaking only what is both true and beautiful. At the end of the week, write down three true, beautiful things that you have spoken.

Praying with the Word

Dear God, creator of all beauty, author of love and goodness, shine into my heart and into the hearts of all. Show me your truth and help me to live what is true. May your glory be alive in me so that those you put into my life may also be made brighter. Teach me not to hide what you have given me, but open my heart to your love and joy. Thank you for the treasure you have given me to hold. Amen. Alleluia.

2 Corinthians 12:1–10

Perfect in Weakness

Opening to the Word

Bring with you to your prayer space something that you find comforting: a favorite sweater, some peaceful music, a mug of hot cocoa, a beloved picture. Spend a few moments before God's word, the Bible, enjoying this comfort. Don't try to pray or to think, just let yourself relax in God's company.

After a few moments, offer a prayer of thanksgiving to God, preferably aloud. Give thanks specifically for those things, persons, events, and places that you hold dear in your heart.

The Word of God

Take the Bible into your hands, and hold it a moment. Remember that you hold the love of God freely given to you. Remember that it is good news, a word of power and strength but also of tenderness and compassion. Remember that this word disturbs, excites, brings life, speaks hope, reveals the truth, and calls people together. Remember that once planted in your heart, it will sprout and grow there.

Read aloud 2 Corinthians 12:1–10. After you have read it, add these words: "Thanks be to God."

Pause for a moment. Do you particularly recall one word, phrase, or sentence from this passage? If so repeat it aloud.

Reflections on the Word

"'Power is made perfect in weakness.' . . . Whenever I am weak; then I am strong."

Perhaps we could be forgiven for skipping over these verses, being frustrated by them, or ignoring them altogether. However, because he was blinded by the light of Christ, Paul's life and preaching were marked by such paradoxes. His path brought him closer to God, to himself, to the Gospel, and to death. Enemies pursued him, friends doubted him, and strangers attacked him. And he had to admit that he was neither perfect nor blameless himself.

A moment of failure happened to me quickly and quietly, but I have felt it ever since. As I emerged one day from our parish chapel, where we had been having a prayer service, Anne, one of the parish workers, told me someone had been looking for me. He had said his name was Frank. He had waited awhile for me, then had gone away just a few moments ago. He had asked Anne to tell me he had gone to detox. I was frustrated that I had missed him, and now I had no way to reach him because he had no phone or address. I didn't even know his last name. I could only wait and hope he would come back.

Frank had been dropping in to see me semiregularly for several months. I had come to know him as a deep and deeply hurt man. He had tried to commit suicide because of his addiction to drugs. He wanted to be free of his addiction, but he was terrified to tear himself away from it. He had even robbed us one night while we were at prayer in order to finance his drug habit. Now I had been unavailable at a moment when he needed me, and I knew I could do nothing about it.

I had missed an opportunity to be part of his healing. Questions nagged at me, too. Did he really go to detox? Did he become lost in the city streets again? I have never seen him since. I pray for him always, but I can do nothing for him.

At times it seems we are set up for failure. We simply are unable to do what is demanded of us. In these times I have wondered about the paradox Paul presents here in this Scripture passage. Paul, a man of strength, fire, and determination, calls his failure or weakness a stake piercing his flesh, an angel of

Satan that is beating him. Even so for years Paul has been proclaiming the Gospel, not only in spite of hardships and limitations but sometimes most powerfully in the moments of greatest helplessness. Weakness doesn't lead Paul to despair. He doesn't conclude that God has asked the wrong person to do an impossible task or that God has been unfair with him.

For Paul, precisely in this unnamed place of weakness and pain, God promises grace. Paul suggests that if he had not acknowledged his helplessness, God could not have met him there. Paul never discounts or glosses over the reality of suffering and pain. On the contrary he often dwells on them quite descriptively, but he can bear to do so because they are pale in comparison with the strength and truth of God's love, which was revealed to him fourteen years before.

God never leads Paul or us to a place of despair or hopelessness or sends us alone to confront the darknesses of our life. Over and over in the Bible, God demonstrates divine love, faithful presence, and constant help for us. God's deepest desires for us are joy, peace, and communion. But if we cannot admit our weaknesses and our failures, we might start thinking that we don't need God. The more we can learn to bring even our failures before God, the more we will be able to feel the power of that mysterious and tender love.

God is the way and the truth. Humility is the virtue of admitting the truth that God has blessed us with all that we are—fearfully and wonderfully made, but vulnerable and weak. Encountering our vulnerability, failures, weaknesses, and sinfulness allows us over and over to recognize the truth: "'[God's] grace is sufficient,'" but God's grace enters into our life only when we ask for it, when we acknowledge that only God's grace gives us enough light to scatter the darkness. Then we too can sing the good news of love and declare with Paul: "'Power is made perfect in weakness.' . . . Whenever I am weak; then I am strong."

The Word in Action

• Each day this week, reserve five minutes to stop everything you are doing and simply give these minutes to God, repeating slowly and attentively, "Whenever I am weak; then I am strong."

• Name a weakness in yourself (physical, mental, emotional, or spiritual). Find a rock and, with a marking pen, write the name of this weakness on the rock. Now, take a sheet of wrapping paper and write on it these words: "'My grace is sufficient for you.'" Wrap the rock in the paper, and keep it where you will see it the last thing at night and the first thing in the morning.

• Name a strength in yourself. Take a sheet of paper and write a letter to God. Tell God what this strength is, give thanks for it, and tell God how you would like to be able to use it to serve someone.

• Find or draw a picture of a person who irritates you or with whom you are in conflict. Keep this person consciously in prayer all week. At the end of the week, take the picture and draw or write on the back of it one thing you find beautiful about this person.

• Do you know one person of faith, a person whom you trust? If so, write down one of your failures or weaknesses—your "thorn." Put the sheet of paper in an envelope and give it to this person. Ask her or him to hold this problem in prayer for you.

• What is one gift or talent or skill with which God has blessed you? Pick just one. This week watch for three opportunities to use it in the service of someone else. Each time you see an opportunity, thank God for this gift and for your ability to use it.

Praying with the Word

God, my God, you have made me as I am. You know me through and through, my strengths and my weaknesses, my limitations and my desires. Let me thank you for the gifts you have given me. Let me serve you in any way you ask. Let me go beyond what I think I am capable of. Lead me to places I would not choose for myself but which you choose for me. Forgive me for the times I have failed; forgive me for being afraid to try again. Thank you for the faithfulness of your love, which will never let me go. Amen. Alleluia.

Ephesians 5:8–20

The Light of Love

Opening to the Word

Leave your prayer space dark. Aloud, silently, or in song, ask for the spirit of God to be present with you in this unlit place. For a few moments, let yourself feel the darkness.

Now, ask God to take you to a time, an event, or a circumstance that has become a burden to you, a dark place in your life. Feel the hopelessness and helplessness of this burden.

Here, even in this darkness, you are not alone. As you had courage to enter into the darkness, take courage again now. Show your burden to the living God. Ask God to hold it for you.

From the darkness light one candle or turn on one small light. Let the light shine on you. Observe how it affects the room, the things around you, and your own skin.

As the light shines into the darkness, so invite God to shine into your dark place. Let this quiet light be present to your burden. Now God bears it with you.

Remain in the light as long as you need to. Then, make a prayer of thanksgiving to God. Your prayer may be as simple as, "Thank you!"

The Word of God

Turn to Paul's Letter to the Ephesians. Read aloud chapter 5, verses 8–20.

Recall, even jot down, any word or phrase that lingers in your mind, anything that surprises you or seems strange to you, anything that irritates or puzzles you, and any word that particularly consoles you.

Read the passage again. Would you like to linger a moment with any particular words or phrases? If so stay with them, and let them dwell in your heart.

When you are ready, read the following reflections.

Reflections on the Word

The beauty and optimism of this passage are in keeping with Paul's whole letter to the church at Ephesus. This epistle overflows with the love of God, the love that called us into existence. This optimism, this overwhelming sense of the glory and wonder of God, is more remarkable given the circumstances in which Paul writes.

Tradition has it that this letter was written late in Paul's life, probably from Rome, where he was imprisoned. Rome was the center of the Western world. The new faith that would be called Christianity was tiny, hidden, and officially treated with contempt or alarm. The love of Christ that so dramatically changed Paul's life had also led him into great suffering and dark places, including prisons. Yet, from within these dark places, Paul proclaimed the light of God.

This optimism comes from Paul's certainty that God's love is not overpowered by the dangers and problems of life. Being in love with God doesn't mean pretending there is no pain. On the contrary it means knowing that suffering cannot overcome God's love. This love, Paul declares, is so much a part of us that it was given to us before the foundation of the world. It makes us holy and blameless. It makes us God's own children.

We were in darkness, and Paul asks us if we can believe that this darkness is past. Further, Paul declares that we are light, that God's love is real, and that the fundamental reality of our life is love. This really is good news!

But this love, Paul reminds us, brings a responsibility and a challenge. God calls us to be our real selves. We belong wholly to love when we turn away from the darkness of despair, fear, violence, or anything else that holds us captive.

"'Sleeper, awake! Rise from the dead, and Christ will shine on you,'" Paul cries out. He writes to encourage the Christian community and also to teach them, to call them to a better life. Real love does not allow others to wander in darkness but helps them learn to live a new way: "Live as children of light."

Thus, we redeem our time by our life in Christ. This compelling command is given by Paul as good news for the whole world. The more we turn to God's love and light, the more the whole world will be illuminated, transformed, indeed, redeemed. Paul, the Ephesians, and we are given the privilege of participating in the healing, redeeming work of Christ. God will show us how our love and our light can transform the world.

Even while Paul reminds the Ephesians to bear the good fruit of a moral life by being "careful then how [they] live," he concludes by urging them to celebrate the light by singing joyful hymns and "making melody" to God in their heart. The good news leads to a good life, a life worth celebrating.

The Word in Action

• Choose a hymn or write a song that celebrates God's love. Let this hymn be part of your week. Sing or hum it whenever you get a chance, but especially when you find yourself clinging to darkness.

• Ask God to show you this week the ways that you cling to darkness instead of allowing yourself to be transformed.

• List a few of your behaviors that lead you into darkness or at least into the shadows: small lies, moments of sloth, bitter retorts. When you feel yourself heading into the shadows, try to remember this passage, especially Paul's advice to "'rise from the dead, and Christ will shine on you.'"

• When you face decisions this week, even relatively minor ones, pause and recall this admonition of Paul: "Try to find out what is pleasing to the Lord," what is "good and right and true." Ask God directly, "What do you want of me at this moment?" Act accordingly.

• Choose one person who you feel could use some light. Pray Paul's prayer for this person whenever you think of him or her: "Grace to you and peace from God" (Ephesians 1:3).

• This week watch for moments of goodness, right living, and truth—in yourself and in other people. You might even keep a log of these moments. At the end of the week, offer a special prayer of thanks to God for these "fruit[s] of the light."

Praying with the Word

God, you bring light to my life. Thank you for always being here with me. Help me to know that no darkness is too dark for you and that I cannot go anyplace where you do not already love me. Mark me with the seal of your spirit, that I may never be separated from you. Teach me to bask in the brightness of your love, this love that has been prepared for me before the foundation of the world. May my life bring light to your world. Amen. Alleluia.

Philippians 3:7–14

Wanting

Opening to the Word

Bring to your prayer space one blank sheet of paper and a pen. For five minutes sit in silence, focusing on the blank page. When the five minutes are up, as quickly as you can, try to recapture all the thoughts you chased away during the five blank minutes. Jot them down randomly.

Add to these thoughts ten other things that you think about often: duties, worries, people, upcoming events, things that have happened lately, things you should be thinking about, things you don't want to think about. Write them just as they come. Don't pause to reflect on each one.

Ask God to hold these things for you during this prayer time. Place these thoughts into the hands of the One who loves you, as you rest the sheet of paper next to your Bible.

The Word of God

Open the Bible to Paul's Letter to the Philippians. Philippi was an important city, founded by Philip of Macedon, father of Alexander the Great. Paul wrote from prison to thank his friends there for their help, to give them news about people they knew, to encourage them, and to tell them more about the faith. This is a short letter, only four chapters.

Take a few moments to look through Philippians. You might want to look at Paul's opening greeting (1:1–2) or his final greetings (4:21–23). You can read Paul's own news (1:12–26) or his affectionate words about his friend Timothy (2:19–22). You can find out about the people who received this letter by reading Paul's personal advice to them (4:2–9), his thank-you for the help they gave him (4:10–20), or the special prayer he makes for them (1:3–11). If you want to enjoy one of the church's earliest and most treasured ways of expressing its faith, read the hymn Paul quotes to them (2:6–11).

Receive this piece of mail that is written to you and to the whole church. Then, turn to chapter 3 and read aloud verses 7–14.

Reflections on the Word

"Is there something you want?" Martha turned, startled. A well-dressed clerk with a plastic smile was looking at her expectantly. In the time it took Martha to open her mouth, an array of things she wanted flashed through her brain in no particular order. Not many of them had to do with items in the shop.

Of course she wanted countless things. Some were things she was working her way toward: a career, a better place to live, a new car. Some were things she wanted all the time, because even when she got them, they didn't last: a meal, a smoke, a good night's sleep. Some were distant dreams: to see the Taj Mahal, to write a novel, to find that special relationship.

While the clerk waited, hoping to find out where he might make a sale, Martha thought about how much of her life she spent wanting. How lightly the word *want* is used, she thought. Sometimes I want wrong or unattainable things. Sometimes my wants cause me to do things I'm ashamed of later. Sometimes I don't know what I should want. Why do I spend so much time wanting when I already have so much?

The clerk starting looking around for another customer. Martha, meanwhile, continued thinking. Even amid all these wants of mine on all these different levels, beneath them all, is something I really want—my true desire. By this point in Martha's reflections, the sales clerk had latched onto someone else.

Usually when we shop, we just get what we want or make do with what is available and go home again. Today's passage from Paul urges us to reflect on what we truly want, deep down. Paul knows now what his real desire is. He has seen something for which it is worth paying the highest price. He runs toward it, he tells the Philippians, as a runner runs toward the finish line. He is certain that he will find it, or rather, that it will find him. Indeed, it is his already and cannot be lost.

Paul has not earned the prize, and he never could be "good" enough to receive it. It is given. Paul's prize is the gift of love, the presence and power of love—a love that has pursued him all his life, a love that calls him upward, as the victorious runner is called up to receive his prize.

Paul calls his old ways and beliefs rubbish, because they held him back from the living God. Once he loosened his grip on his old beliefs, he was able to be given his heart's desire. He let go of what was behind him, and he reached out to what was ahead, coming toward him.

"I want," Paul writes from prison, "to know Christ and the power of his resurrection and the sharing of his sufferings by becoming like him in his death, if somehow I may attain the resurrection from the dead." Again, Paul presents us with a paradox. Christ has made Paul his own, but Paul will "press on toward the goal" of knowing Christ. Paul realizes that God's love is infinite and that even if we have accepted God's love, the journey is not done. Every day offers us new ways of understanding and encountering the living God. So Paul presses on toward the goal.

Paul knows that pressing on requires detaching ourselves from the things that we cling to: money, prestige, power, sex, vices. We know these are obstacles between us and God, chains that bind us. But other, subtler, kinds of chains also exist.

One evening, in the hall of the inner-city church that I was working for, we had a twilight retreat. Some fifty church members gathered for prayer and reflection. The participants that night came from a wide spectrum of classes, backgrounds, ethnicities, and levels of education.

At one point we gathered in small groups for reflection on a Scripture passage. The passage had to do with the gifts God gives to us. The persons in the group were each asked to name one personal gift they had, one way in which they themselves were a treasure. In our group everybody struggled with the question. And then there was Carol. When her turn came to speak, Carol was absolutely defeated by the question. She blushed, sweated, looked intently at the floor, and refused to look up. She simply could not identify anything good in herself—not aloud to us and, I suspect, not in silence to herself.

After a few moments' silence, the pastor, who happened to be at our table, spoke. He leaned forward and said: "Carol, you are one of the kindest, most generous people I have ever met. Whenever anything needs to be done, you are there to do it. When everybody else is getting angry and upset, you are peaceful. Carol, you are a light in our parish."

The pastor knew Carol well. He wasn't making all this up. Carol, through it all, was still unable to look up or to speak, but the tears in her eyes spoke for her. She glowed under the truth of his words.

I have often recalled that moment. Carol, it seemed to me, was not bound by greed, lust, pride, or the familiar temptations. But she was bound by her own idea of herself, by her conviction that she wasn't worth much. And maybe she was bound, too, by the values that the rest of us tend to place on things. She wasn't rich, powerful, or beautiful. She had no university degree, successful career, or important friends. She wore hand-me-down clothes and did menial work. In worldly terms she had little value. And that was the way she felt. That self-image held her captive.

When, like Paul, we finally turn toward God and let go of our chains, we may be surprised to learn what they are. Carol couldn't free herself of her chains. The pastor, who knew a different way of valuing things, was able to free her for a moment from what she clung to. For the moment she was able to be freely in the presence of God's love; she was able to know Christ through the love of another. It was a privileged moment.

Beginning to acknowledge what we really want and what we actually cling to requires the grace of courage, real prayer, and the compassionate presence of the One who loves without condition. Like Paul we need to remember that Christ Jesus is already running to meet us, already coming to give us the prize. In God's grace we need only press on.

The Word in Action

• Leave in your prayer space the sheet on which you captured your thoughts at the beginning of this session. Anytime this week, when you are bothered by worries or anxieties, recall this sheet being held in its place, held safe in God's love. Ask God directly to care for your thoughts. Every night before bed, thank God for the care and love with which your thoughts are being held.

• Find a way to care for one other person's wants this week. Your care may be quite tangible or it may be completely hidden or spiritual. Ask God's guidance in choosing the person and in trying to provide what she or he wants.

• Memorize today's passage, either the whole of it or one or two verses that particularly speak to you. Speak these words aloud at least once daily over the next week.

• In prayer ask God to show you one thing to which you cling. Try to name it—fear, despair, anger, bitterness—whatever it may be. Ask aloud and deliberately to be freed of this chain. During the week be attentive to its presence. Whenever you feel it binding you, call on God, perhaps using Paul's words: "Rubbish. . . . I press on!"

• Ask God to help you with something that is behind you, but of which you haven't quite managed to let go. You may use these words of Paul's to help you: "I have suffered the loss of [these] things . . . in order that I may gain Christ."

• Find or buy some small, tangible thing that you want. Wrap it up and keep it in your prayer space. Try to describe for yourself the goal toward which you are running, the prize that you want to receive. During the week concentrate on letting God give you this prize. At the end of the week, take the treat you bought for yourself and either give it away or share it with someone.

Praying with the Word

God of my heart, take my heart and make it your own. Give me the desire of my heart, and teach me to receive it. Free me of the chains that bind me, and let me reach out to what is ahead of me. Be my desire. Be all I want. Be my life. May my desires, my wants, my life be yours. Help me to treasure what you give me. Thank you for the abundance and generosity of your love for me, and thank you for giving me what I really need. For I am yours. Amen. Alleluia.

Colossians 3:1–4

Back to Life

Opening to the Word

Today, bring the Bible into your quiet space, along with a candle and one other thing that will help you to focus on God: a picture of a beloved person or place, an icon, a flower or another thing of beauty, incense, or a keepsake from a holy time. Place this item, the candle, and the Bible where they will be above you and out of reach, but within your sight, when you sit down.

Darken the room as much as you can, and light the candle. Sit with the word of God above you. Pray aloud, either in your own words or using a prayer you know—perhaps the Lord's Prayer—and make the sign of the cross.

Now, alone before God, take a few moments to look into the places in your heart that need to be healed, whatever you are afraid to show God but need God to see. Allow God's light to illumine the dark places, for it is the light of love.

The Word of God

Look up to the light burning beside the word of God. Stand up so that you can reach out and take the word to yourself. Take the light too, and sit down again.

Hold the Bible. Hold the word of God's love in your heart, even in the dark places where you have asked God to walk with you. Receive this word and let it dwell with you.

Open your Bible to the Letter to the Colossians, chapter 3, verses 1–4. Read these verses aloud slowly.

Paul did not found the Christian community of Colossae, his friend Epaphras did. This letter is closely related to the Epistle to the Ephesians, which comes a little earlier in our Bible, and also to Philemon, the shortest and the last of the collection of Pauline letters. Imagine how challenged and consoled the Colossians must have felt when they received this letter.

Reflections on the Word

Coming home from my errands one day led me up a street I had not walked since I moved out of that part of town more than ten years before. I felt that I had moved on and up and could bask in a life with fewer cockroaches, and with mice instead of rats. I wasn't paying much attention to where I was, just thinking over the day's events and heading for the nearest subway station.

A few paces ahead, a tall, thin figure in purple staggered and swayed. A drunken man, I thought in the corner of my mind. The purple figure crumpled. I walked over to the fallen form, which turned out to be a gaunt old woman. Her head was tilted against the wheel of a car; her legs were splayed on the sidewalk.

I leaned over to ask her if she was all right. She mumbled something about wanting to go home or not wanting to go home. Her cracked voice and slurred speech made it impossible to tell which. "Can you stand?" I asked. She reached out a hand, but I couldn't raise her. The thought occurred to me: Who am I, that I should be able to raise another person?

She had greasy hair loosely tied with a string, a filthy purple shirt, sagging polyester pants. And a face—granite-edged, slack-mouthed, purple also, leather-tough, eyes pale and vague. Reeking. The face of Christ?

"I want to go home," she said. Or perhaps it was, "I don't want to go home," or maybe both. Then, "Who the hell are you?" "I'm Mary," I said. "Where did you come from?" "I walked up the street," I replied.

"Leave me alone. I want to go home." She reached out her arm again, and again I tried to raise her up. But she couldn't or wouldn't stand. I crouched down beside her. She threw up on the sidewalk and took my arm again, trying to get up. "I'm too damned drunk to get up," she said. "I want to go home."

I put my arm around her. She gave up trying to stand and lay down on the sidewalk like a baby, her head pillowed on my knee. A person. A hopeless case. A drunk on the sidewalk. "Leave me alone," she said. She moved away from me and lay still.

I thought of stories that friends had told of trying to help street people and being stymied at every attempt. I thought of the number of bodies curled up on benches that I had walked by that very day. I thought of the expense of calling the police to help someone who couldn't be helped. I thought of the arrogance of reaching down to a fallen person. I thought. But she was lying with her head in the gutter.

From a pay phone, I called emergency. Very soon ambulance attendants arrived. I forced myself not to apologize for making them waste their time on a useless, expensive errand. They put on latex gloves as they walked up.

We all stood over her where she lay, unsure what to do with her, unable to see any way of improving her situation. A police officer arrived. Now there were four of us looking down at her. The others discussed whether to take her to detox or to a hospital or to her apartment. None of the choices were particularly appropriate. Nothing was appropriate. She belonged nowhere.

The police officer picked up her purse. That roused her. She clung to her purse as he took it, dragging along the ground behind it, almost losing her baggy pants in the process. One of the ambulance attendants quietly pulled them up for her. The officer emptied her purse and found her identification. "Are you Joyce?" he asked. "Yeah, I'm Joyce. What the hell is going on here?" She crammed the contents back into her purse.

He was still reading her ID: "Sarnia," he said, "that's a nice place." She was sitting on the road now between two parked cars, complaining. One of the ambulance attendants turned and told me that they didn't need me. I walked away.

A hopeless case and a completely unimportant one. No way to help. They did what they could. I walked on through this city neighborhood with its decrepit buildings, shifting ethnic population, and garbage in the streets. And garbage on the sidewalks.

We have a clean city with relatively little poverty or violence. At least the ambulance and the police responded to my call. At least they were willing to try. At least they treated her like a living being. And I, having caught a stray glimpse of the hopelessness that we are immersed in but need never see, and having been for the moment overwhelmed by it, and having walked away, who am I?

And who is she? This fallen woman, this child of God—Joyce from Sarnia. Where are you now, Joyce? Who cares for you? Does Christ, the Christ I claim to know, cradle you like a child in its mother's arms, speaking your name in love, counting the hairs on your head? And does this God look up from that embrace and see me and ask me who I am?

Paul lived and died two millennia before Joyce fell on the sidewalk in an urban slum. But her story, I suspect, would not have surprised him. His letter to the Colossians openly names some of the darkest realities of human life. He describes falseness and illusion, hypocrisy and injustice. He knows it is possible to reduce faith to merely following rules or keeping up appearances, to be held captive by human self-sufficiency, as though Christ did not exist. Paul speaks of greed, evil desires, impurity, and other ways that people are led astray.

Paul is not afraid to face the reality of sin and evil in the world. He knows that humans, including Christians, are fully capable of sin and that the closer we get to Christ, the more inescapable this truth is. Indeed, the darkness of the world seems at times overwhelming. Over and over again, Paul and each of us come up against the limits of our own ability to love, even to love those who are easy to love. Evil seems so abundant, so powerful, and so much in control.

Paul's reply is, "Seek the things that are above, where Christ is." Once again Paul tells us to focus on Christ, the One who stands in the midst of sin and evil and claims victory over them. Focus, Paul says, on "Christ who is your life."

How are we to do that? To look at Joyce is to look at Christ. To look at the one next to us is to look at Christ. To look at ourselves is to look at Christ. After all, "looking above" means looking beyond mere appearance. It means looking to the heart of life, which is filled with God's holy presence, to see life as God does—with infinite love.

"When Christ who is your life is revealed, then you also will be revealed with him in glory." To look at Christ is to know ourselves as with Christ in God.

The Word in Action

- This week keep the Bible in a high place, a place where you have to look up to see it. Put with it some of the sacred things you have had in your prayer space. Whenever you look up at it, pray these words of Paul's: "[Let me] seek the things that are above, where Christ is."

- Choose something that you frequently need to look at, such as a clock, or something that you commonly use, such as the closet door. Write one word or phrase from today's Scripture passage of which you would like to be reminded. Place it beside the item you have chosen so that when you look at that item, you are reminded of Paul's words.

- Concentrate this week on looking, really looking, at the people with whom you come in contact. Look them in the eye when you speak to them. Listen not only to the words they say but to who they are. After each encounter give God thanks for these people.

- Take some time to name for yourself the things that are important in your life. Write each one on a slip of paper and collect all the slips in a box. Put the box in your prayer space. During your prayer time, commit your life and all that is important to you to God's keeping.

- Find one place in your life that is in need of help. Ask God to show you one step you can take toward healing this hurt and to give you the courage to take it.

- Identify one thing you can do to help someone else or society. Ask God to show you one step you can take to be of assistance. This may be something quite simple and practical, for instance, providing an hour of free baby-sitting or a precooked meal for a neighbor who has small children. It may be the smallest of steps, such as phoning your church or a volunteer agency and asking what needs it has. For now take this one step, and put it into God's hands.

Praying with the Word

God, you are my light, my love, and my joy. When I am in need of healing and forgiveness, hide me in your embrace. When I don't know how to help, give me wisdom. When I am able to turn to you, show me your compassion and love. Help me to see in others the face of Christ and to show them the face of Christ in all that I am and do. I ask your help for those who are in difficult situations, especially these for whom I pray. . . . Raise my mind and heart to you. Thank you for the faithfulness of your love. Amen. Alleluia.

1 Thessalonians 4:13–18

To Dream a Little

Opening to the Word

Bring to your prayer space, along with your Bible and whatever else you usually have there, a cloth of some kind: some colored material that you like the look or feel of, a small tablecloth, even a scarf. Lay out the cloth as though you were setting a table, so that it is prepared to receive something. Beside it put the Bible and the other things; have the candle ready to be lit.

Then, go out for a walk. If that is impossible, choose another low-key pleasant activity, such as petting your cat or dog, watering the plants, or cutting vegetables. Don't put expectations on or thought into the activity, just let it clear your mind a little.

When you come back, light the candle, sit comfortably, and rest a little with your God. When you have spent some time together and you feel relaxed, take a moment to let God dream in you, or let yourself dream in God. You can be quite free in this and peaceful. Show God the beauty that rests in your own heart, and let God take you further in.

When you feel ready, proceed to the word.

The Word of God

Pick up your Bible, open it to Paul's letters, and leaf through them: Romans, Corinthians, Galatians, Ephesians, Philippians, Colossians, Thessalonians, and so on. All the people these letters are addressed to are brought together here. They have been gathered into a communion with Paul, with the Apostles, and with you. Christ unites them.

Turn to the First Letter to the Thessalonians, probably the earliest writing in the Christian Testament. Thessalonica was an important city located on sea and land routes. Paul spoke of Christ to the citizens, some of whom were changed by hearing this word. So a church was founded there. As he continued his travels, Paul wrote back to this community.

Take a moment to acquaint yourself with this letter. Then, turn to chapter 4 and read aloud verses 13–18.

Reflections on the Word

They came—from different places, for different reasons, but they came: politicians, beggars, merchants, mothers, soldiers, ordinary business people. All of them gathered in a place called Thessalonica. All of them felt drawn to one voice, one word: a word that spoke to their heart and touched a dream.

Can one dream really be dreamed by many people? This is what happened to the people of Thessalonica. They stopped being strangers and became a community.

Paul and his friends came to Thessalonica and spoke through words and actions the Good News that they had learned. They shared the spirit of God that enflamed their hearts. The word that Paul brought touched the hearts of the Thessalonians and gathered them together. It brought present hope, a promise that was already being worked out in their lives. Already they tasted joy.

It is to this church community that Paul now writes. He asks about them, responds to their questions, encourages them, and praises their faith. He helps them to understand the new Way to which they have been drawn. And yet, these Thessalonians are sad. Paul's letter to them is also a word of comfort.

The Thessalonians have tasted the promise of new life. Outwardly, perhaps, they look just the same; inwardly they know a transforming joy. They have felt the love of the One who is present with them and with whom they will be fully united. Yet, full union with Christ, the fulfillment of the promise, still awaits. So their joy is mixed with grief, much like it was for two friends of mine.

Gerry and Sue had always wanted a family, and they rejoiced in their three children. A present joy. But they also dreamed about who their children would become, how they would grow, and what their lives would be like. A present joy, leading to something greater.

Before the youngest child was three years old, Gerry died. Left with the three children, Sue experienced present grief and future grief. Present grief, in being parted from one she loved, and future grief, in knowing that they would never experience together the fulfillment of their children's lives. It was a promise that could never be fulfilled.

Like Sue and Gerry, the Thessalonians received a promise for the future. They had joy already in knowing Christ and one another in Christ. While they lived in the world, they also awaited something greater still. Their shared hope made the Thessalonians an extremely close-knit community. Looking forward to something and sharing that anticipation with others creates a bond among those who eagerly wait.

Yet, now, this cherished hope, this promise of fulfillment and of a joyful meeting with Christ, seems to have been dashed to the ground. Before the fulfillment is accomplished, some of the Thessalonians have died. How can Christ's promise be fulfilled now? How can he bring about the joy of which he gave them a taste when some of them are no longer there? How can that hope come true when all means of accomplishing it appear to be gone?

The Thessalonians seem to have had a certain idea of just how the fulfillment would look. They had settled in their own minds how God would give them what had been promised. Perhaps they had envisioned themselves faithfully waiting in Thessalonica as Christ came back among them and brought them home to himself.

God's ways are much bigger than ours, and though they call us beyond ourselves, we still tend to picture them in terms we can understand. It's part of being human. Sometimes we pin our hopes on our own ideas of how things will happen. We forget that God is full of surprises and brings about the word in ways that we could never imagine or hope for. When things don't happen the way we expect, we are tempted to wonder if God's word hasn't been broken.

Providentially, the Thessalonians have a friend in Paul. Paul knows that God's promise is never false and that the present life is not the whole story. He tells the Thessalonians not to grieve "as others do who have no hope." He doesn't expect them not to grieve, but he does expect them to cling to their hope. They haven't begun to understand the fullness of that hope. Their hope is still, in some ways, limited to their own terms of reference. It hasn't been fully opened by the living presence of God, who transcends death and life.

Paul paints a picture of how life and death intersect and of the richness of God's promise, which is more beautiful than what we can see, just as a mountain lake is more beautiful than the postcard we saw that drew us there. God will be coming among us with a clarion call, the call that made the fishermen leave their nets, the tax collector his money, and the prostitute her pain. God's voice calls us, Paul says, not to hopelessness, defeat, or death. It calls us to a new relationship, deeper, higher, wider, more exalted, and more encompassing than the one we have begun to glimpse on earth.

God can and will bring about the promise in ways that we cannot fully understand, but in which we can participate. God doesn't call us to hang around putting up with this life and waiting to die. We already can live in God's promise because we have this hope, because God is working this miracle in and for us. Our life already is filled with a meaning that is greater than we know.

Don't be afraid to hope, Paul urges Christians. Don't be fooled by appearances. Don't be grieved like those who have no hope. Let hope make you free.

The Word in Action

- This week set aside a few minutes each day to dream of God's promise. Simply enjoy the freedom and beauty of the dream itself. At the end of the week, offer a special prayer of thanksgiving for this time spent with God.

- Recall a promise that you have made but have not yet kept. Act on it.

- Visit a dying person or someone who is grieving a death. Or simply send a note and a prayer to someone in this situation, perhaps a person in your church community. Draw on the words of Paul to help you in what you say.

- In your church make a special effort to speak to someone you don't know or to whom you have never spoken. Try to talk to that person as a family member rather than as a stranger.

- Take some time to reflect on death, either in prayer or with someone else. What is the Christian belief about death? What is the hope we have? Read 1 Thessalonians 4:13–18 again, and pray with it this week to help you in this reflection. If you have questions you can't answer, take them to someone in your church who can help you.

- "Encourage one another," Paul exhorts the Thessalonians. This week listen for moments in which others are giving you encouragement. Watch for moments in which you can help encourage someone else.

- Do you sometimes limit God, what God can do, in your mind and heart? If so converse with God, asking for a larger vision of who God is and what God can do for you and for the world.

Praying with the Word

God of all glory, you have promised us fullness of life, communion with one another, and joy in your presence. Help us to live this promise in each moment of our life. Fill us with hope so that we can bear witness to you by our way of life. When we don't understand your ways, when moments of despair come, hold us close. When we are sad, remind us of the true hope from which we can never be parted. When death touches us, show us how to encourage one another. Teach us to wait faithfully and in love and eagerness. You are our eternal joy. Amen. Alleluia.

1 Peter 5:6–11

Cast Your Cares

Opening to the Word

Find a stone. Take some time to find one that you like the look and feel of. In your prayer space, hold the stone in your hands. In song or in quiet, ask the spirit of God to be present with you.

Close your eyes, and feel the stone in your hands—feel its weight, its shape, and the smoothness or roughness of its surface. Call to mind a time or place of suffering in your life. Hold in your heart this time of suffering, just as you hold in your hands the stone you have found.

Take the stone and lay it in your prayer space. Take the suffering and lay it in the hand of God, who longs to take it from you.

Now, sit a few moments with your hands empty. They are held by God.

The Word of God

Take up your Bible. Find the last letter attributed to Paul, which is addressed to Philemon. Turn to the Epistle to the Hebrews, whose authorship is unknown. After Hebrews come several short letters with personal names as their titles: James; 1 and 2 Peter; 1, 2, and 3 John. These are written not to particular communities, as were Paul's letters, but more generally to the churches. Tradition associates them with the Apostles James, Peter, and John.

Turn now to the First Letter of Peter. Read the first verse, which attributes the writing to the Apostle Peter and addresses it to the "exiles of the Dispersion."

Before you read today's passage, call to mind the countless Christians who have walked the earth since these words were written in the first century. Recall the Christians in your own life—friends, family, or people in your faith community. This letter is addressed to us all.

Turn now to chapter 5 of 1 Peter and read verses 6–11.

Reflections on the Word

On this bitterly cold Wednesday afternoon in late January, the winter sunshine was fading. Headlights and street lamps came on. Cars and buses jammed the streets.

Inside our little drop-in center were warmth, hot coffee, and a gathering of people. Some were preparing the evening meal that was open to anybody who was hungry for food and companionship. Some were getting ready for the evening prayer that would begin in an hour's time. Everyone was welcome, no one was obliged to attend. A blast of frigid air burst in with a shabby couple. He was a big man with a ragged beard, a shapeless gray coat, and run-down boots. She was a slight woman with stringy brown hair, large flashy earrings, and cigarette-stained fingers. They were regulars at our drop-in center and often brought others with them. Today they had two small children in tow.

The couple wandered around finding friends to talk to. The two children, who had never been here before, stood silently by the door. One looked to be about six years old, the other perhaps four. Going over to invite them in, I saw that neither of them was wearing hats, mittens, or boots, only light jackets and shoes without socks.

I took the younger boy and sat down with him. His fingers and face were dead-white, his lips blue. He couldn't speak, but he sat motionless on my lap while his older brother explained that they had walked several blocks to come to us. Someone brought a hot drink for the little boy, others brought warm coats and blankets.

We were sitting in a warm place, but the child couldn't warm up. His skin was icy. His brother, who recovered fairly quickly, told us his own name was Kyle and his brother's name was Ryan. Kyle went away to amuse himself, but he came back frequently to see how his brother was doing and even offered him some of the cold drink he had obtained.

In big and small ways, each of us has been afflicted with pain and sorrow that is not of our own making but which comes into our life. People tend to be uncomfortable with sufferers, for words can't take away the suffering. Confronted with suffering and helpless in the face of it, we are unable to avoid our own limitations. I realized that although I could do a little to relieve Ryan's suffering, he was just one of the legions of homeless, hungry, and abused children in the world about whom I could do nothing. How powerless we are.

First Peter is written in such circumstances. The author knows the suffering that his readers have endured. They became Christians joyfully, but their entry into new life has brought hardship and pain. Their faith has torn them from friends, family, and financial security. Peter is confronted with pain and sorrow that he cannot undo or pretend away. And the situation is not likely to improve, for their faith makes them a minority and a community, difficult for those outside the community to understand.

Peter's response doesn't minimize the depth of their suffering. He dares to enter into their suffering and bear it with them. He knows what it means to suffer, too.

As I was sitting with the child Ryan that cold winter night, John came in and saw us. John was also a familiar face at the drop-in center. He lived pretty much on the streets, doing odd jobs, writing poetry, and talking philosophy with me from time to time. John came over, looked at Ryan, looked at me, and said, "There's only one way to warm this child." He stripped off his leather jacket, knelt in front of me as I held the boy, and unwrapped Ryan's feet, which were enfolded in blankets. He took the bare feet and put them under his armpits. With his hands he rubbed the child's ankles and calves. He knelt there, his tattooed arms working to warm a child he had never met before, his scarred face intent upon the face of Ryan. For several moments we remained that way.

Slowly, Ryan, who had begun to shake in my arms, was being penetrated by the warmth. At last he grew relaxed and calm. Eventually, he got up from my lap and went away to be fed. When I saw him later, I discovered a beautiful blond boy with pink cheeks, rosy-red lips, and a rambunctious nature.

John's touch and his body's warmth healed this boy and brought him back to life. John was by no means a self-sufficient, successful, educated, or even socially acceptable person. He was probably the last person most of us would have thought to ask for help. But he did know what it was to suffer. He knew what it was to be cold and alone, to need and not to have, to be powerless. And he gave what he had, his own presence.

Presence is perhaps the greatest gift one person can give to another. Presence that receives, accepts, and cares for the reality of the other person well defines compassion—to suffer with another person. This is what John offered Ryan and what Peter offers his fellow Christians. "Know," Peter writes to them, "that your brothers and sisters in all the world are undergoing the same kinds of suffering." Peter tells them that their suffering can unite them in the One in whose name they gather.

Peter urges his fellow Christians to throw their cares on God, who is longing to bear them. Where evil, fear, and humiliation are strongest, this is exactly where God is most present. No suffering is beyond the reach of God. Christ himself has already entered into our pain. No pain is too great for his love, no suffering is beyond his reach, no person exists that he does not care for.

Peter dares us to take the truth of this unfathomable love even into the hardest places—into our own suffering and into the suffering of others.

The Word in Action

- This chapter began by asking you to recall a moment of suffering. Spend some prayer time this week with that suffering. Recall what happened. Ask God's help now for the pain you still bear, or give thanks to God for the ways your pain has been taken from you.

• Take with you the stone you placed in your prayer space. All week keep it with you where you can hold it and touch it, praying, "You, Christ, will 'support, strengthen, and establish' me." At the end of the week, give the stone and an explanation to someone you know who is in pain.

• Say these words aloud: "God, you care for me, and I throw my cares upon you." Repeat them several times until they are firmly in your memory. Repeat them again every morning and every night this week. Be alert this week to even the smallest moments of pain, doubt, or helplessness in yourself or in those around you. When such moments come, repeat the words.

• Read again today's passage from 1 Peter. Choose one phrase or sentence that you think would give comfort or help to a person in pain. Write it out carefully on a card, or draw or illustrate it. Keep this card for a time of sorrow, your own or someone else's.

• In your prayer time this week, ponder a Scripture passage in which Jesus on the cross cries out to God (e.g., Mark 15:34).

• Be aware this week of physical touch. Give thanks to God for the gift of touch, and ask God to show you when to reach out to someone and when to receive the touch of another.

Praying with the Word

God, I am sometimes weighed down by the worries of my life. I put before you today my sufferings and sorrows. I put before you also the sufferings of people whom I know. Receive them in your love, and teach us how to receive what you give. Help me to let go of what I bear, casting it on you instead of trying to carry it all myself. Remind me, in the darkest moments, that all my cares are handled by you. Put me in order, make me firm, strengthen me, establish me. Show me how to care for others and how to point them toward your love. Guard us always in the compassion of your love for us. Amen. Alleluia.

2 Peter 1:16–21

The Morning Star Rises

Opening to the Word

Open your Bible to the beginning of the Christian Testament, then set it in your prayer space. Place beside it a new, lit candle. Sit with your hands resting on your legs, palms up. Breathe deeply. Concentrate a few moments on these deep breaths.

Pray aloud: "Come, Spirit of truth. Give light to my heart."

Ask God to show you, in your heart, a place of doubt, a time when your faith wavered or even collapsed. Recall it quite specifically, if you can.

Now, blow out the candle. Remain for a few moments aware of the presence of the Holy Spirit.

The Word of God

Read again the first words of the Christian Testament: "An account of the genealogy of Jesus the Messiah, the Son of David, the Son of Abraham." The Bible in your hands offers you the Way, the Truth, and the Life. Receive them now.

Turn to the Second Letter of Peter, almost at the end of the Christian Testament. It is directed generally to Christians living in Asia Minor, struggling to be faithful to the word they have received and taken into their heart.

Read now the words of hope and promise and encouragement in chapter 1, verses 16–21.

Reflections on the Word

Have you ever wished that God would just speak plainly, put up a big neon sign, write your name on it, and say: "Here! Here's the way!" So often we seem to be stumbling in the fog. Where's the light that will help us? Do we ever find any certainty on the path of faith, in the life of the Spirit?

In this passage Peter is saying, "Pay attention to this. This is the place to look." He explains that the Good News is no "cleverly devised myth." Rather, he stands as an eyewitness to Christ's "majesty." Christ Jesus, the Messiah, came in flesh and blood to reveal the infinite love of God for us in terms that even Peter could understand.

Often, we doubt our faith. At times we doubt even the visible things. We wonder, fret, and second-guess. That's why Peter writes this way. He knows that it's difficult to live a life of faith. He knows that we need to encourage one another and to recall the presence of God in our life. It's a presence that transforms, but even this transformation can be confusing and can raise new doubts.

Don't worry, Peter says, the transformation really happened. Plenty of other people heard and saw it too, and the Scriptures help to keep us in that truth. The flame is in you, and so you yourself have become evidence, a witness to the truth of God's love.

One afternoon I spent a couple of hours waiting in a packed airport for a friend whom I had come to meet. Because the airplane was late, I had leisure to observe the people crammed together in the lounge. Although all were so different from one another, they all had this in common: they were waiting. Some were resigned, some impatient, some tired, some tense. All were waiting.

Soon, I noticed that something was happening over and over again. As I watched the people, suddenly one of the faces would become bright, focused, attentive. The one this person was awaiting had arrived. I didn't need to see the one arriving to know this; I knew from the transformation in the person who was waiting.

The event Peter recounts, the "lamp shining in a dark place," is a little like that. At the Transfiguration on the mountain (see Matthew 17:1–8, Mark 9:2–8, Luke 9:28–36), several of the disciples became "eyewitnesses of his majesty." They witnessed the presence of God in a way that they would never forget. Because they had been walking with Jesus, they had been changed. But at the Transfiguration, the disciples were able to see in a new way what had always been there to see—the "honor and glory [of] God." And the evidence was in themselves, in the way that they were lit up and transformed by the light.

The greatest, most powerful witnesses of the good news of God's love are often the least likely. After all, we remember Peter as first among the Apostles, but most people in his time just saw a rough–hewn, illiterate, mule-headed fisherman. Lamps burn in unexpected places.

One night in my parish, we had an all-night vigil. During the night between Holy Thursday and Good Friday, the church was open for prayer. The parish stood in the middle of a business district lit brightly by neon and traffic. Inside, the church was lit only by a vigil candle. All was still, but something was happening.

A little distance away from me was a woman, one of the most faithful churchgoers in the parish and one of the loneliest people I have ever met. She was perhaps fifty years old, divorced, living alone in a tiny apartment, and working many hours at a tedious job that supported her and helped finance periodic visits with her two sons, neither of whom lived in the same city as her. She was always available to help serve coffee or to clean up after events or to stuff envelopes and answer phones. Many people avoided her because she was a nonstop talker, and once you were caught, it was hard to get away. That was Diane.

When I arrived at the vigil around midnight, only Diane was there. I sat and watched her in the light of the one candle. As the church grew darker and the night colder, it seemed to me that two flames burned in that church with intensity and faithfulness: the vigil candle and Diane in prayer. Both were still burning when the first light of the new day began to creep in through the windows of the church. The memory of both has remained with me ever since.

Peter cries, Pay attention! Even in the midst of darkness, see the lamp. Even in the midst of doubt, receive the truth. Christ's flame can burn in your heart and transform it. Then, you will become evidence of God's love. Then, every moment of your life will become a flame of love. Then, you will learn to see the flames of love all around you, and your hidden acts and quiet moments will burst forth like shooting stars.

Like the disciples on the mountain, we cannot walk with Christ and not be changed.

The Word in Action

- Recall the moment of doubt that you offered to God in the opening prayer. Write on a sheet of paper a statement of faith, expressing to God your trust and belief. Add one verse from today's Scripture passage. Sign the sheet and date it, and put it in an envelope addressed to yourself. At some point on your spiritual journey, when you need encouragement, open the letter and read it.

- This week, observe the faces around you. When you are speaking with someone, whether it's a friend, your spouse, or a bank teller, look closely at that person and recall the presence of Christ in her or him. When you part from that person, say a prayer for her or him.

- Carry with you this week a small pad of paper and a pen. Every time you hear a word of hope spoken or see evidence of love, jot it down on the pad. At the end of the week, read your jottings and give thanks for them.

- Tell one person whom you see this week one way that God's presence has affected your life.

- One day this week, get up before dawn. Sit by a window and place a lit candle in front of you. Now, do something you enjoy that can be done right where you are: reading, knitting, writing, relaxing, drinking coffee, listening to music. Stay until you see the darkness begin to lighten. Then, say aloud the Lord's Prayer.

• Make a painting, sketch, or sculpture that expresses for you this phrase of Peter's: "The morning star rises in your hearts." Give it to a person who is experiencing a time of pain or sorrow.

Praying with the Word

Glorious God, you are the light of the world. You have promised that we will not wander in the dark but will always have the light of your love. Thank you for your faithfulness. Forgive me for times of doubt, despair, or fear. Be with me in these dark times. Fill my life with your love so that I may light the way for others. Receive all that I have and all that I am. Let me never be parted from you. Amen. Alleluia.